African-American Musicians That Changed Music Forever

100 Legendary Artists That Created the Soundtrack of our Lives

To : Ann

Thank you so much for your support. Please enjoy reading the Book.

Michael A. Carson
Matthew A. Carson

Double Infinity Publishing
P. O. Box 55 Grayson, GA 30017

Printed in the United States of America

African-American Musicians That Changed Music Forever

Co-Author: Matthew A. Carson
Research Assistant: Matthew A. Carson
Content Editor: Shenika H. Carson
Cover Design: Double Infinity Publishing
Design Director: Shenika H. Carson

ISBN-13: 978-0578775142
ISBN-10: 057877514X

Double Infinity Publishing books may be purchased in bulk at a special discount for sales promotion, corporate gifts, fund-raising or educational purposes. For details, contact the Special Sales Department, Double Infinity Publishing, P.O. Box 55 Grayson, GA. 30017 or by email: DoubleInfinityPublishing1@Gmail.com.

DEDICATION

As a Father and Son writing team, my co-author Matthew and I would like to dedicate this book to my beautiful wife Shenika, who continues to inspire us, thank you for all of your love and support.

To the next generation of African-African musicians who continue to shatter records, influence, inspire, and affect social change through their musical talent.

Other Publications By Author: Michael A. Carson

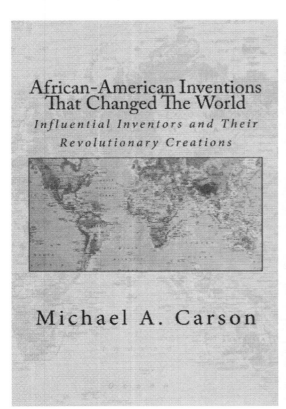

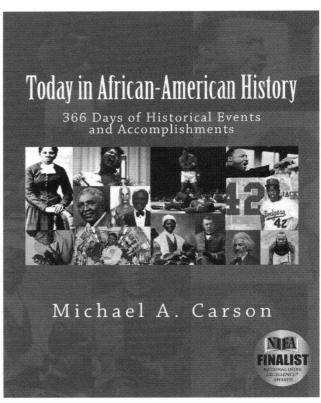

Double Infinity Publishing

Contents

INTRODUCTION

Throughout history, African-American musicians and artists have made a profound impact in music, they have given sound and voice through a wide variety of musical genres. Universally they have expressed emotions that is shared through faith, passion, joy, comfort, and injustice through songs that speaks directly to the heart and spirit.

Many of these performers have the power to influence, inspire, and affect social change through their musical talent. Their personal stories and experiences have transcended time and encouraged several generations to continue singing, dancing, preaching, and perform with musical instruments. Over the past two centuries these experiences have become part of a cultural identity.

The incredible men and women featured in this book are responsible for creating some of the most iconic songs ever recorded in the history of music. Their trailblazing sounds have been synonymous in the inception of several musical genres such as Gospel, Blues, Jazz, Soul, Rock & Roll, R&B, Disco, and Hip-Hop, to name a few. Their timeless musical treasures continue to enrich and endure our culture, history, spirit, and soul.

While recognizing the impact African-American musicians have made worldwide, through inspiring millions to sing, dance, express their faith, and march for justice, the federal government officially declared the month of June as "African-American Music Appreciation Month," which was originally established in June, 1979.

In an effort to honor the countless musicians, singers and composers who have played an integral role in crafting America's soundtrack as well as contribute to every musical genre ever conceived, each year during the month of June, the country recognizes and highlights the contributions African-American artists have made throughout history, and the impact their music has made in our society and the world.

Michael Jackson

Major Awards	Wins
Grammy Awards	15
American Music Awards	26
Golden Globe Award	1
Billboard Music Awards	5
MTV Video Music Awards	28
World Music Awards	26
Guinness World Records	39
Presidential Medal of Freedom	3

Major Hall of Fame Inductions

Rock & Roll Hall of Fame
Grammy Lifetime Achievement
Grammy Hall of Fame
Songwriter's Hall of Fame
Hollywood Walk of Fame

Known as the "King of Pop," Michael Jackson (1958 - 2009) was a dynamic force as the pre-teen frontman of his chart-topping family group "The Jackson 5," he then pursued a solo career and moonwalked his way into superstardom. Over the course of his legendary career, he emerged as a global icon. More than 40 years after its debut, his album "Thriller" remains one of the best-selling albums of all time. Between his supple tenor and mesmerizing footwork, Jackson reigns as the ultimate showman who continues to influence future generations with his signature dances and timeless music.

Singer, Songwriter, Dancer and Philanthropist, commonly referred to as the "King of Pop," Michael Jackson is regarded as one of the most significant cultural figures of the 20th century, and one of the greatest entertainers in the history of music. His contributions to music, dance, and fashion, along with his publicized personal life, made him a global figure in popular culture for over four decades.

As the 8th child of the Jackson family (who were signed to Motown Records), he made his professional debut in 1964, along with his elder brothers Jackie, Tito, Jermaine, and Marlon as a member of the "Jackson 5." In 1971, Jackson decided to embark on a solo career. He rose to solo stardom with his debut album "Off the Wall" (1979), by the early 1980's, he became a dominant figure in popular music.

Jackson is credited with revolutionizing and transforming the music industry with the creation of his music videos including, "Beat It," "Billie Jean" and one of his many signature videos "Thriller." His Thriller album became and currently remains the world's best-selling album, and the first album to be certified 33 times multi-platinum, having shipped more than 33 million units.

Despite the global success and massive earning power of Thriller, Jackson was adamant about not getting complacent with his career. Described as "The most Anticipated Album in History," his next studio album "BAD" debuted at No. 1 in the United States and a record-breaking 24 other countries, it then became the second best-selling album of all time (behind Thriller).

Every world tour that Jackson performed on during his career would sell out with record breaking crowds, his "BAD" tour holds the world record for the highest grossing tour in history, earning a staggering $125 million in profits. His follow-up concert series "Dangerous" and "History" world tours were attended by more than a combined total of 10 millions fans.

Jackson is also regarded as one of the largest philanthropist in history, all of profits from his Dangerous tour were donated to various charities, including his own "Heal the World Foundation." He is also recognized as "The Most Successful Entertainer of All Time" by the Guinness World Records, having sold an estimated 350 million records worldwide.

Tina Turner

Major Awards

Major Awards	Wins
Grammy Awards	8
American Music Awards	3
Billboard Music Awards	9
MTV Video Music Awards	3
World Music Awards	9
NAACP Image Award	1
Guinness World Record	1

Major Hall of Fame Inductions

Rock & Roll Hall of Fame
Grammy Lifetime Achievement
Grammy Hall of Fame
St. Louis Walk of Fame
Hollywood Walk of Fame
Postage Stamp Honor - Grenada

Well-known for her trademark legs and energetic stage presence, Tina Turner (1939 -) began her legendary career performing with musician Ike Turner in the 1950's. They became known as the "Ike and Tina Turner Revue," achieving popular acclaim for their live performances and recordings. She split from the group in the 1970's stepping into the solo spotlight achieving massive success with her 1984 album "Private Dancer." She rose to prominence that same year with the release of her now signature anthem, "What's Love Got to Do with it." Turner is noted for her energetic stage presence, powerful vocals, and career longevity, as she became one of the world's top recording artist.

Singer, Songwriter and Actress, often referred to as "The Queen of Rock & Roll," Anna Mae Bullock, who is known professionally as Tina Turner was one of the most popular international performers of the 20th century. While born in the United States, she later became a permanent resident and citizen of Switzerland. Growing up in Nutbush, Tennessee, she began singing at the age of 7 in the Nutbush Spring Hill Baptist Church choir. As a teenager, she quickly immersed herself in the St. Louis R&B scene, spending much of her time at "Club Manhattan," where she met Rock & Roll pioneer Ike Turner in 1956.

Turner rose to stardom as part of the "Ike and Tina Turner Revue" before launching her own successful career as a solo performer. In 1984, she released her debut solo album, "Private Dancer," which was a triumph, both critically and commercially, she rose to prominence that same year with the release of her now signature anthem, "What's Love Got to Do with it," selling more than 20 million copies worldwide.

Shortly after, Turner went on a 47 city world tour, known as the "Ageless Rock Diva," she gave electric performances that encompassed 40 songs each night as well as a continuous barrage of video and sound wizardry. In 1988, while on tour, Turner shattered the world record for the largest paid audience for a solo artist, when she performed in Rio de Janeiro, Brazil in front of 180,000 fans. According to Guinness World Records, she has sold more live concert tickets than any other solo performer in history.

Throughout her legendary career, Turner has sold over 200 million records worldwide. In the United Kingdom, she became the first female artist to have a top 20 hit song in 6 consecutive decades, she is also the first female artist in history to garner concurrent Grammy nominations for Pop, Rock, and R&B genres.

The motion picture, "What's Love Got To Do With It," starring actress, Angela Bassett, was released in 1993, tells Turner's life story. In 2019, she celebrated her 80th birthday and was also portrayed in the live Broadway version of her incredible life story, "Tina: The Musical," starring, actress, singer and dancer, Adrienne Warren. The Musical was also featured in the cities of London, Hamburg and Utrecht.

Turner has also enjoyed a career as a successful actress, starring in motion pictures such as the 1975 Rock musical "Tommy," the 1985 action film "Mad Max Beyond Thunderdome," and the 1993 film "Last Action Hero."

Sam Cooke

<u>Major Hall of Fame Inductions</u>

Rock & Roll Hall of Fame
Grammy Lifetime Achievement
Grammy Hall of Fame
Songwriter's Hall of Fame
R&B Hall of Fame
Hollywood Walk of Fame

Known as the "King of Soul," Sam Cooke (1931 - 1964) was one of the most popular Soul singers in history. He began his career as a Gospel singer in 1950 after replacing R. H. Harris as lead singer of the Gospel group the "Soul Stirrers." Cooke is credited for bringing Gospel music to the attention of a younger crowd of listeners with his smooth, soulful tenor. His transition into solo career as a Soul singer lead to such unforgettable songs such as "Twistin' the Night Away," "Cupid," and "A Change Is Gonna Come." He was among the first African-American performers and composers involved with the business side of the music, he founded both a record label and a publishing company as an extension of his career as a singer and composer. His pioneering contributions to Soul music contributed to the rise of other artists such as Aretha Franklin, Al Green, Curtis Mayfield, Stevie Wonder and Marvin Gaye. Cooke has also popularized the likes of musical legends Otis Redding and James Brown.

Singer, Songwriter, Civil-Rights Activist and Entrepreneur, commonly known as the "King of Soul" for his distinctive vocals, Sam Cooke is regarded as one of the most influential figures in the history of popular music. Growing up in Chicago, Illinois, Cooke joined a neighborhood Gospel group at the age of 14, he befriended fellow Gospel singer and neighbor Lou Rawls, who sang in a rival Gospel group. Cooke then joined the "Soul Stirrers," a premier Gospel group of the 1950's, he electrified the African-American church community nationwide with a spiritual vocal style that soared.

In 1957, he decided to leave the group in order to pursue a solo career as a Soul singer, his decision to convert over to popular music had tremendous implications within the African-American musical community. There had been a long taboo against such a move, but Cooke broke the mold. He reinvented himself as a romantic crooner in the manner of Nat King Cole. His strength was in his smoothness. He wrote many of his best songs himself, including his first hit, "You Send Me," which shot to No. 1 on all charts in 1957 and established him as a superstar.

Cooke was essentially a spiritualist, even in the domain of romantic songs. When he released the singles, "Twistin' the Night Away" and "Cupid," he did so with a delicacy previously unknown in Rock music. Even though he was no longer a Gospel artist, he sanctified and glorified his Gospel heritage and forged new paths. In 1961, he become the first African-American artist to establish his own record label, "SAR Records." He also distinguished himself as an independent businessman, heading his own publishing, recording, and management firms.

His refusal to sing at segregated concerts led to what many have described as one of the first real efforts in civil disobedience, and helped usher in the new civil rights movement. His landmark song "A Change Is Gonna Come" has been voted as one of the "Greatest Songs of All Time," it was selected for preservation in the Library of Congress, with the National Recording Registry deeming the song "culturally and historically important." Cooke was also close friends with boxing legend, Muhammad Ali, he produced Ali's recording titled "The Gang's All Here." Many of Cooke's compositions have been featured in several motion pictures and television shows. His music heavily influenced entire generations of Soul performers.

Aretha Franklin

Major Awards	Wins
Grammy Awards	18
American Music Awards	4
NAACP Image Awards	3
Presidential Medal of Freedom	1

Major Hall of Fame Inductions

Rock & Roll Hall of Fame
Grammy Lifetime Achievement
Grammy Hall of Fame
U.K. Music Hall of Fame
R&B Hall of Fame
Gospel Music Hall of Fame
NAACP Hall of Fame
National Medal of Arts
Hollywood Walk of Fame

Known as the undisputed "Queen of Soul," Aretha Franklin (1942 - 2018) took Soul music to unprecedented heights beginning with her 1967 breakout song "Respect." Her father, Reverend Clarence La Vaughan "C. L." Franklin was a national renowned Baptist Preacher. She soon began singing in front of his congregation, her musical gifts became apparent at an early age. Largely self-taught, she was regarded as a child prodigy. As a gifted pianist, Franklin's impact on several music genre's are unsurpassed, her powerful voice was bred from Gospel, Blues and Jazz.

Child Prodigy, Singer, Songwriter, Actress, Pianist, and Civil Rights Activist, who was famously known as the "Queen of Soul," Aretha Franklin has been electrifying fans with her soulful vocals for over five decades. Growing up in Detroit, Michigan, her singing career began at the age of 14, recording some of her earliest tracks at her father "C. L." Franklin's church, which were released by a small label as the album "Songs of Faith" in 1956.

Franklin also performed with C. L.'s traveling revival show, where she then taught herself how to play piano without knowing how to read music. While on tour, she befriended Gospel legends such as Mahalia Jackson, Sam Cooke and Clara Ward. In 1960, with her father's blessing, Franklin embarked on a secular music career and traveled to New York City to pursue a recording contract. After being courted by several labels, including "Motown" and "RCA," she signed with "Columbia Records."

Hitting her stride over the next two decades, she created a string of hit records that would later become enduring classics. During the 1960's, Franklin was considered a symbol of African-American pride through her music. Her songs "Respect," "You Make Me Feel Like a Natural Woman," "Young, Gifted, and Black," and "Think" became anthems reflecting the country's growing concerns over racial injustice. In 1966, she signed with "Atlantic Records" which gave her more creative control, she began revolutionizing Soul music by creating a sound all her own. In 1987, she became the first woman inducted into the Rock & Roll Hall of Fame.

Franklin has also performed at three U.S. Presidential Inaugurations, in 1977, she performed "God Bless America" for President Jimmy Carter, 16 years later, she headlined a two-hour concert during President Bill Clinton's inauguration, and in 2009, she electrified a crowd of more than one million in attendance with her performance of "My Country, Tis of Thee" at President Barack Obama's inauguration.

Rolling Stone Magazine ranked Franklin as No. 1 on its list of the "100 Greatest Vocalists of All Time." Billboard also named her "The Greatest Female R&B Artist of All Time." Throughout her legendary career, Franklin has received honorary degrees in music from several universities including Harvard, Princeton, Yale, and the New England Conservatory of Music.

Ray Charles

Major Awards   **Wins**

Grammy Awards   17
NAACP Image Awards   3
Presidential Medal of Freedom   2

Major Hall of Fame Inductions

Rock & Roll Hall of Fame
Grammy Lifetime Achievement
Grammy Hall of Fame
Songwriter's Hall of Fame
NAACP Hall of Fame
National Medal of Arts
Hollywood Walk of Fame
Honored on U.S. Postal Stamp

Commonly referred to as "The Genius" for his skills as a Singer, Songwriter and Composer, Ray Charles (1930 - 2004) set off a firestorm in the 1950's with his first No. 1 single, "I've Got a Woman" and his game changing combination of R&B, Gospel and Blues. Charles career spanned over five decades, he racked up such classics as "Hallelujah I Love Her So," "What'd I Say" and "Hit the Road Jack." Born as Ray Charles Robinson, he dropped his last name to avoid confusion with the popular legendary Boxer at the time "Sugar" Ray Robinson. His remarkable talent inspired an entire generation of musicians and his creativity extended to the many instruments that he touched.

Singer, Songwriter, Pianist and Composer, often referred to as "The Genius," Ray Charles was one of the first African-American artists to merge the Blues with Gospel genres, which paved the way for R&B music. Growing up in Albany, Georgia, he contracted glaucoma at the age of 5, which eventually left him blind by the age of 7.

In order to help teach him to be self-sufficient, his mother sent him to the St. Augustine School for the Deaf and Blind in Florida. There he learned how to read music in Braille as well as to play both Classical and Jazz music on the piano, saxophone, trumpet, and, clarinet Charles always maintained that his visual impairment never hindered his career in any way.

In 1947, he moved to Seattle, Washington, and started a band, he worked in night clubs singing Nat King Cole style songs, he then became close friends with legendary music producer Quincy Jones. Soon after, he then began to wear sunglasses while performing, this action began the trend for all blind musicians to do the same.

His fusion of Gospel and R&B helped to create a new musical genre known as "Soul music." By the late 1960's, Charles began entertaining the world of Jazz, cutting records with members of the "Modern Jazz Quartet." Fellow musicians began to all refer to him as "The Genius," an appropriate title due to his versatility and never just working one style, he blended and beautified all that he touched. Charles was an innovator in business as well as music, after joining "ABC Records," he made history by becoming the first African-American musician to own the masters to his recordings, he was also granted artistic control on his music.

Presidents, political dignitaries and members of royal families have all recognized Charles as a "Musical Icon." The King and Queen of Sweden chose him to receive a Polar Music Award, which is the country's most prestigious award. Rolling Stone Magazine ranked Charles as No. 2 on their list of the "100 Greatest Vocalists of All Time," and No. 2 on their list of the "100 Greatest Singers of All Time." The motion picture, "Ray" starring Actor/Comedian, Jamie Foxx opened in 2004, tells his life story. Foxx won an Academy Award for "Best Actor," and the film won several other awards.

James Brown

Major Awards	Wins
Grammy Awards	3
American Music Award	1
BMI Icon Award	1

Major Hall of Fame Inductions

Rock & Roll Hall of Fame
Grammy Lifetime Achievement
Grammy Hall of Fame
Songwriter's Hall of Fame
BET Lifetime Achievement
Hollywood Walk of Fame

As an iconic figure who is globally recognized as a Singer-Songwriter, known as "The Godfather of Soul," "Soul Brother No. 1," and "The Hardest-working Man in Show Business," James Brown (1933 - 2006) is one of the most influential musicians of all time. As a major figure of 20th century music and dance, his career spanned more than six decades. He brought African-American pride into the musical conversation. His gritty, street-edged vocals, (a cross between singing and talking) also laid the foundation for Rap/Hip-Hop. As an iconic global figure, his high-energy concerts, capped by his dizzying dance moves and infamous cape routine, set the tone for future generations of entertainers such as Michael Jackson and countless others. Rolling Stone Magazine ranked Brown as No. 10 on its list of the "100 Greatest Vocalists of All Time." He is also the most sampled artist in history.

Singer, Songwriter, Dancer, Producer and Bandleader often referred to as the "Godfather of Soul" and "Soul Brother No. 1," James Brown is considered to be among the greatest artists in the history of popular music and the most sampled musician of all time. In a career that lasted over six decades, he influenced the development of several music genres.

In 1955, Brown began his career as a Gospel singer, he became a member of the group "The Gospel Starlighters," who later changed their name to "The Famous Flames," a group founded by Bobby Byrd. The Flames immediately hit the road after releasing their album "Live at the Apollo," performing hit ballads such as "Try Me" and "Please, Please, Please," touring the Southeast opening for legendary musicians such as B.B. King and Ray Charles.

In addition to producing, writing and recording hit records, Brown toured relentlessly. He performed five or six nights a week throughout the 1950's and 60's, a schedule that earned him the title "The Hardest-Working Man in Show Business." Brown was a flashy showman, incredible dancer, and soulful singer, his concerts were hypnotizing displays of exuberance and passion that left audiences wanting more. His saxophonist, Pee Wee Ellis, once said, "When you heard James Brown was coming to town, you stopped what you were doing and started saving your money."

During the 1960's, Brown recorded many of his most popular and enduring hit singles including, "Papa's Got a Brand New Bag," "I Got You (I Feel Good)" and "This is a Man's World." Along with its unique rhythmic quality, his signature "Papa's Got a Brand New Bag" is considered the first song of a new genre, "Funk," an offshoot of Soul and a precursor of Hip-Hop.

On April 5, 1968, the day after Dr. Martin Luther King Jr.'s assassination, with riots raging across the country, Brown gave a rare televised live concert in Boston to promote peace, in an attempt to prevent more rioting. His effort succeeded, young Bostonians stayed home to watch the concert on TV and the city largely avoided violence. A few months later he wrote and recorded his groundbreaking single "Say It Loud: I'm Black and I'm Proud," a protest anthem that has unified and inspired generations of activist. Brown was a large contributor of the civil rights movement and a staunch believer in exclusively nonviolent protest.

Prince

Major Awards	Wins
Grammy Awards	7
American Music Awards	6
Billboard Music Awards	7
MTV Video Music Awards	4
Academy Award	1
Golden Globe Award	1
NAACP Image Awards	4
Soul Train Awards	2
Brit Awards	7

Major Hall of Fame Inductions

Rock & Roll Hall of Fame
R&B Hall of Fame
U.K. Music Hall Of Fame

Prince (1958 - 2016) was a remarkably talented musician who first captured the world's attention with his numerous album releases in the 1980's. Originally named Prince Rogers Nelson, later in his career he was referred to as "The Artist Formerly Known as Prince," or "The Artist." He was a rare composer who could perform at a professional level virtually on any instrument that was required, a considerable number of his songs featured him performing this role. His innovative fusion of R&B, Funk, Jazz and Rock put the him and his hometown of Minneapolis, Minnesota on the map in 1978 with his debut album "For You."

Singer, Songwriter, Producer, Dancer, Actor and Filmmaker, Prince is regarded as one of the most talented Popular music artists of his generation, his music integrated a wide variety of styles, including R&B, Funk, Jazz and Rock. After taking an early interest in music, he began playing the piano at the age of 7, he also mastered the guitar and drums by the time he joined his first band at the age of 14.

Early in his career, he released of albums "Prince" (1979), "Dirty Mind" 1980) and "Controversy" (1981), which were produced, arranged and composed entirely by Prince in his home studio in Minneapolis, Minnesota. Along with his band "The Revolution" he then released the popular albums "1999" and "Purple Rain," which cemented his superstar status with No. 1 hits like "When Doves Cry" and "Let's Go Crazy."

In 1984, his classic album, "Purple Rain" also served as the soundtrack to the motion picture he released of the same name. The film which co-starred singers Apollonia Kotero and Morris Day grossed $70 million at the box office, it also garnered an Academy Award for "Best Original Song Score." The album was certified 13-times platinum, it sold over 25 million copies worldwide, making it the third-best-selling soundtrack album in history. In 2012, the album was added to the Library of Congress National Recording Registry list of sound recordings.

Throughout most of his career, Prince was a prolific songwriter, he wanted to release material as soon as it was ready, this idea clashed with his record company's policy of releasing only a single album each year. He had a backlog of more than 500 unreleased songs within his famous studio vault that were piling up. He gave many songs to other performers; some of whom were recorded at Paisley Park (the studio and record label he established in suburban Minneapolis).

In 1993, he announced that he would no longer go by the name Prince, but rather a "Love Symbol" which was made up of the gender symbols for a man and woman, the symbol was a rebellion against his record label, Warner Bros. In 2000, after his contract expired, Prince went back to using his original name, which allowed him to innovate new ways to sell records as an independent artist. Throughout his legendary career, he sold over 100 million records, ranking him among the best-selling music artists of all time.

Marvin Gaye

Major Awards	Wins
Grammy Awards	2
American Music Award	1
NAACP Image Awards	3

Major Hall of Fame Inductions

Rock & Roll Hall of Fame
Grammy Lifetime Achievement
Grammy Hall of Fame
Songwriter's Hall of Fame
R&B Hall of Fame
Hollywood Walk of Fame
Honored on U.S. Postal Stamp

Singer, Marvin Gaye (1939 - 1984) embarked on his solo career in 1962, having already played drums for Smokey Robinson, "The Miracles" as well as several other Motown groups. He was one of the main singers that created the "Motown Sound" of the 1960's, first as a session performer and later as a solo artist. His Motown hits included "How Sweet It Is, (To Be Loved By You)" "I Heard It Through the Grapevine," and "Mercy Mercy Me," as well as countless classic duets with Mary Wells, Kim Weston, Diana Ross and Tammi Terrell. Gaye influenced an entire generation of contemporary artists, his albums have been listed as inspirational, powerful and noteworthy.

Singer, Songwriter, Producer and Actor, Marvin Gaye is one of "Motown Records" most versatile performers. He helped to shape the sound of Motown in the 1960's, first as a session player and later as a solo artist with a string of hits, earning him the nicknames "Prince of Motown" and "Prince of Soul."

Throughout his childhood, Gaye often found peace in music, mastering the piano and drums at a young age. Until high school, his singing experience was limited to church revivals, but soon after he developed a love for R&B and Doo-wop that would set the foundation for his career. In the late 1950's, Gaye joined a vocal group called "The New Moonglows."

Gaye's early years at Motown were full of behind-the-scenes successes. He was a session drummer for Motown legends such as Stevie Wonder, "The Supremes," "The Marvelettes" and "Martha and the Vandellas." Advancing as Motown's own renaissance man, he went on to break into the Top-10 for the first time in 1962 with his solo single "Hitch Hike." Gaye recorded some of the most revered love anthems of all time, including his signature hit single "Let's Get It On." The song became his second No. 1 Billboard hit, cementing his crossover appeal once and for all.

Throughout most of the 1970's, Gaye was on tour, collaborating or producing. He recorded duets with Mary Wells, Kim Weston, Diana Ross, and, most famously, with Tammi Terrell. Together, "Marvin and Tammi" reigned as the "Royal Couple of R&B" and scored major hits with "Ain't No Mountain High Enough," "Your Precious Love" and "Ain't Nothing Like the Real Thing," among others. Although still a popular solo artist, Marvin Gaye's 1968 recording of "I Heard It Through The Grapevine" sold 4 million copies and was the top-selling Motown single at the time.

In 1970, inspired by escalating violence and political unrest over the Vietnam War, Gaye wrote the landmark song, "What's Going On." The single was released in 1971 and became an instant smash, its success prompted Gaye to take even more risks, both musically and politically. When it was released in the spring of 1971, the "What's Going On" album served to open Gaye up to new audiences while maintaining his Motown following. His later recordings influenced several contemporary R&B sub-genres, such as "Quiet Storm" and "Neo Soul."

Ella Fitzgerald

Major Awards	Wins
Grammy Awards	13
American Music Award	1
NAACP Image Award	1
Presidential Medal of Freedom	1

Major Hall of Fame Inductions

Grammy Lifetime Achievement
Grammy Hall of Fame
Oklahoma Jazz Hall of Fame
National Medal of Arts
Hollywood Walk of Fame
Honored on U.S. Postal Stamp

Regarded as "The Queen of Jazz," Ella Fitzgerald (1917 - 1996) was the most popular female Jazz singer in the United States for more than half a century. Her voice was flexible, wide-ranging, accurate and ageless. She could sing sultry ballads, sweet Jazz and imitate every instrument in an orchestra. Fitzgerald was also the first African-American woman to win a Grammy Award. She became an international legend during a career that spanned over six decades. She recorded more than 250 albums, many of which were timeless classics. During her legendary career, she earned the nickname, "The First Lady of Song."

Jazz Singer, who was often referred to as "The Queen of Jazz," and "The First Lady of Song," Ella Fitzgerald was an immensely popular Jazz and song vocalist who is considered to be one of the greatest female Jazz performers in history. From an early age, Fitzgerald harbored dreams of becoming an entertainer, she entered a contest and made her stage debut at the world famous Apollo Theater in Harlem during "Amateur Night." Her singing moved the crowd and she won "1st place prize," her performance helped set her career in motion. Soon after, she met bandleader, Chick Webb, who led one of the most popular swing bands in the country. Webb invited 16 year-old Fitzgerald to join his band as a singer.

In 1935, she recorded "Love and Kisses" with Webb's band and found herself playing regularly at one of Harlem's hottest clubs, "The Savoy." She also put out her first No. 1 hit, "A-Tisket, A-Tasket" (1938), which she co-wrote. Later that year, Fitzgerald recorded her second hit, "I Found My Yellow Basket." Following Webb's death in 1939, Fitzgerald became the leader of the band, which was renamed "Ella Fitzgerald and Her Famous Orchestra," her band began touring with singer, Dizzy Gillespie, she then developed her famous "Skat" singing style (singer improvises melodies).

In 1958, Fitzgerald made history as the first African-American woman to win a Grammy Award, she would also go on to sell more than 40 million records in her career and evolve as one of the most celebrated singers of the 20th century. She then pursued a career in acting, appearing in several motion pictures and guest staring on many popular television shows.

Her musical collaborations outside of her solo career were with some of the greatest musicians in the history of Jazz music, including Louis Armstrong, Duke Ellington, and "The Ink Spots." These partnerships produced some of her best known songs such as "Dream a Little Dream of Me," "Cheek to Cheek," "Into Each Life Some Rain Must Fall" and "It Don't Mean a Thing (If It Ain't Got That Swing)."

Outside of the arts, Fitzgerald had a deep concern for children and those in need. Though this aspect of her life was rarely publicized, she frequently made generous donations to organizations for disadvantaged youths. The continuation of these contributions was part of the driving force that prevented her from slowing down from touring all across the world.

Al Green

Major Awards   **Wins**

Major Awards	Wins
Grammy Awards	11
American Music Awards	1
Soul Train Music Award	1

Major Hall of Fame Inductions

Rock & Roll Hall of Fame
Grammy Lifetime Achievement
Grammy Hall of Fame
Songwriter's Hall of Fame
Soul Train Hall of Fame
BET Lifetime Achievement
Gospel Music Hall of Fame
Memphis Hall of Fame

Al Green (1946 -) has emerged as one of the premiere Soul vocalists of the early 1970's and 1980's. As an unrivaled hitmaker, his extraordinary voice became known to the world through a string of legendary hits such as "Tired of Being Alone," "Let's Stay Together," "I Can't Get Next to You," "I'm Still in Love With You," "Call Me," "Here I Am," "Let's Get Married" and his signature single "Love and Happiness." Whether singing the praises of God though Gospel music or performing his secular hit records, Green remains as one of the greatest Soul singers in history.

Singer, Songwriter, Producer and Actor, Al Green was the most popular performers of Soul music during the 1970's. Throughout his legendary career, he further transformed the essential relationship in Soul music between the sacred and the secular, following the musical and spiritual path of his greatest inspiration, Sam Cooke.

Green started singing professionally at the age of 9, he and his brothers formed a Gospel quartet. They toured the Gospel circuits throughout the South, then began performing in Michigan when the family relocated from Arkansas to Grand Rapids. He then formed a Pop group at the age of 16, they released the single "Back Up Train" which went to No. 1 on the R&B charts. Shortly after, Green decided to pursue a solo career.

In 1968, while on the road in Texas, Green opened for Producer and record label Vice President, Willie Mitchell. Impressed with what he heard, Mitchell signed Green to "Hi Records" of Memphis. As he started working closely with Mitchell, Green's soft phrasing and higher than normal embellishments took Soul music into a new direction. In 1971, he remade the popular hit song by "The Temptations," "I Can't Get Next to You."

Mitchell also produced Green's other huge hits of the 1970's, including the No. 1 "Let's Stay Together" and "I'm Still in Love with You." Along with his ballads, his gifts of long-stemmed roses to female concert-goers and his golden voice, Green became an international megastar. While on the road in 1973, he became born again as a Christian. Despite his revived faith, he continued touring and releasing secular hits as he had previously.

In 1976, Green purchased a church, "The Full Gospel Tabernacle" in Memphis, TN., and began leading services. In addition to becoming a Pastor, he turned back toward spiritual music. As his producer, Mitchell did not want to work on Gospel songs. Green then released his 1977 album, "The Belle Album," which was self-produced.

The new direction his life had taken was evident in the song "Belle," about a man torn between his love for a woman and his love for God. After turning away from the songs that had made him famous, he then became comfortable with both his popular music and his religious vocation. Green's career has spanned more that four decades, he was also ranked No. 14 on Rolling Stone Magazine's list of "100 Greatest Singers of All Time."

Stevie Wonder

Major Awards	Wins
Grammy Awards	25
American Music Awards	2
Academy Award	1
Golden Globe Award	1
Soul Train Award	1
NAACP Image Awards	4
Guinness World Record	1
Presidential Medal of Freedom	1

Major Hall of Fame Inductions

Rock & Roll Hall of Fame
Grammy Lifetime Achievement
Songwriter's Hall of Fame
NAACP Hall of Fame
Hollywood Walk of Fame

Over the course of his five decade career, Stevie Wonder (1950 -) has often been dubbed the "Eighth Wonder of the World." Blind since shortly after birth but blessed with natural gifts as a singer, songwriter and multi-instrumentalist, he is one of the few artists who has successfully transitioned from teen to adult stardom. Signed to Berry Gordy's Motown "Tamia" label at the age of 11, Wonder scored his first Billboard 100 hit at just 13 years old with "Fingertips." During that time, he was known as "Little Stevie Wonder." He then became one of the most creative musical figures of the 20th century with hits like "My Cherie Amour," "I Just Called to Say I Love You" and "Part-Time Lover."

Child Prodigy, Singer, Songwriter, Musician and Producer, Stevie Wonder is regarded as one of the most successful songwriter's and musicians in the history of music. After making his recording debut at the age of 11, he made his first hit song. Wonder then became the first singer to have a No. 1 album as well as a No. 1 single simultaneously.

In 1973, he became the first African-American to win a Grammy Award for "Album of the Year," a feat that he repeated for 3 consecutive albums. He has since gone on to be nominated for a Grammy Award a total of 74 times, the most nominations for any musician in history.

Over the next decade, he had an array of No. 1 songs. In 1976, he released a double album titled, "Songs In The Key Of Life," it was ranked by Rolling Stone Magazine as one of the "Greatest Albums of All Time." The album became the first of an American artist to debut straight to No. 1, where it remained for 14 consecutive weeks.

In 1980, he released the album titled "Hotter Than July," which featured the hit single "Happy Birthday," the song was dedicated to Dr. Martin Luther King Jr. Wonder was one of the pioneers of having the U.S. Government declare Dr. Martin Luther King's birthday a National Holiday. Thanks to his contribution, in 1983, Dr. King's birthday was signed into law as an American federal holiday which is observed on the third Monday of January each year.

In 1985, Wonder became the first Motown artist as well as the second African-American musician to win an Academy Award for "Best Original Song," for the single "I Just Called To Say I Love You" for the motion picture, "The Woman in Red."

During his legendary career, Wonder has sold over 100 million records worldwide, making him one of the best-selling musicians of all time. He also has won 25 Grammy Awards, making him one of the most awarded artist in history. As a "United Nations Messenger of Peace," he has been able to win the rights to publish copyrighted works into formats accessible to the visually impaired throughout the world. He will forever be known as a pioneer in music and a messenger of peace addressing controversies in music in which very few artists have done.

Luther Vandross

Major Awards	Wins
Grammy Awards	8
American Music Awards	9
NAACP Image Award	1
Soul Train Music Awards	5

Major Hall of Fame Inductions

Songwriter's Hall of Fame
Soul Music Hall of Fame
Hollywood Walk of Fame

Luther Vandross (1951 - 2005) was one of the most successful R&B Artists of the 1980's and 1990's, scoring a series of multi-platinum albums containing chart-topping hit singles. Long before he debuted as a solo artist in 1981 with the hit album "Never Too Much," he was well known as a respected singer and entertainer. He contributed his talents as a backup singer, songwriter, and arranger to albums by Chaka Khan, Quincy Jones, and Roberta Flack. As a solo artist he took charge of his music creatively, while arranging and producing his records. Known for his distinctive interpretations of classic Pop and R&B songs, he also possessed a smooth, versatile tenor voice which he used to charm millions of fans with his romantic music.

Singer, Songwriter and Producer, Luther Vandross began his professional career singing commercial jingles and background vocals. He also worked as a vocal arranger, contributing the song "Everybody Rejoice" to the Broadway Musical "The Wiz" in 1972. Vandross then became a background vocalist for Diana Ross, Donna Summer and Chaka Khan, he made his career breakthrough as a featured singer with the studio group "Change." In 1980, he decided to launch a solo career.

Vandross came to the attention of record executives and signed with "Epic Records," which allowed him to write and produce his own material. In 1981, his first album titled, "Never Too Much," sold more than one million copies, its title song was an instant No. 1 R&B hit.

His silky tenor branded him the unofficial "Ambassador of Sophisticated Soul" as his love-themed singles "Stop to Love," "Here and Now," "Dance With My Father" and duets "If This World Were Mine" with Cheryl Lynn, "The Best Things in Life Are Free" with Janet Jackson all were at the top of R&B charts.

During his legendary career, Vandross reached No. 1 on the Billboard R&B album chart a total of 8 times (7 of which were consecutive No. 1 albums). He became one of the most popular artists in the crossover genre called "Urban Contemporary Music." As a producer, Vandross was also responsible for the success on albums for Dionne Warwick and Aretha Franklin, who, along with "The Supremes," greatly influenced his music.

Vandross was commonly referred to as "The Velvet Voice" and was often called "The Best Voice of a Generation," in reference to his exceptional vocal talent, he was also regarded as the "Pavarotti of Pop." Over the course of his 25 year career, he sold over 35 million records worldwide. Rolling Stone Magazine ranked Vandross as No. 54 on its list of the "100 Greatest Vocalists of All Time."

Vandross consistently sold out arenas all over the world, in 1989, he performed 10 consecutive sellouts at Wembley Arena in London, England, solidifying his reputation as one of the most popular live entertainers ever. He imposed his own direction on R&B music while maintaining his passion for romantic songs, along the way he drew a massive fan base.

Josephine Baker

Major Awards	**Wins**
Resistance Medal	1

Major Hall of Fame Inductions

Honored on France Postal Stamp
Honored on U.S. Postal Stamp

Singer and Dancer, Josephine Baker (1906 - 1975) was one of the greatest entertainers of the 20th century. As an American woman she moved to France and became a French citizen, she symbolized the beauty and vitality of African-American culture when she took Paris by storm in the 1920's. She became the first African-American woman to star in a major motion picture, which was the 1927 film "Siren of the Tropics." As a world renowned entertainer and singer, she was also a trailblazer and social campaigner who fought against racial injustice throughout her career. Baker became involved with the civil rights movement and the National Association for the Advancement of Colored People (NAACP). She returned to the U.S. in 1963 for the March on Washington, where she spoke alongside Dr. Martin Luther King Jr. In recognition of her work and activism throughout the years, the NAACP declared May 20th as "Josephine Baker Day."

Singer, Actress, Dancer and Activist, Freda Josephine McDonald, who is known professionally as Josephine Baker is one of the most popular and influential performers of the 20th century. She led a legendary career that illustrates the ways entertainers can use their platforms to change the world. Growing up in St. Louis, Missouri, she joined a theatre troupe at the age of 15, she also married during this time, taking her husband's last name and dropping her first name, becoming Josephine Baker.

In 1919, Baker toured the U.S. with the group "The Steppers," and garnered a reputation as an excellent vocal singer whose dancing ability and comic expression were equally matched. She eventually moved to New York City and participated in the celebration of African-American life and art known as "The Harlem Renaissance." A few years later her success took her to Paris. She then became one of the most sought-after performers, bringing Jazz style music to Paris and becoming well known due to her distinct dancing style and unique costumes. In 1931, Baker released the single, "J'ai deux amours," which became her most successful recording. Although her audiences were mostly Caucasian, her performances followed African-American themes and style.

During World War II, the German Army invaded France, Baker joined the fight against the Nazi regime. She aided French military officials by passing on secrets she heard while performing in front of the enemy. She transported the confidential information by writing with invisible ink on music sheets. When the war ended, she became the first American woman ever to receive French military honors.

Known as a multi-talented dancer and singer, Baker also starred in several major motion pictures released in Europe. After many years of performing in Paris, she returned to the United States. Her return home forced her to confront the same segregation and discrimination she experienced when she was a child in St. Louis. In protest, she denounced her American citizenship and became a French citizen in 1937. As a staunch civil rights activist, her opposition to social injustice was recognized by the National Association for the Advancement of Colored People (NAACP). In 1963, she was one of a few women who spoke at the March on Washington for Jobs and Freedom. Her speech detailed her life and experience as an African-American woman in the United States and abroad.

Issac Hayes

Major Awards	Wins
Grammy Awards	3
American Music Award	1
Academy Award	1
Golden Globe Award	1

Major Hall of Fame Inductions

Rock & Roll Hall of Fame
Grammy Hall of Fame
Songwriter's Hall of Fame
Memphis Music Hall of Fame
Hollywood Walk of Fame

There are not many figures who have exerted a greater influence over the music in the 1960's and 1970's than Isaac Hayes (1942 - 2008). After laying the groundwork for the "Memphis Soul Sound" through his work with "Stax Records," Hayes began a highly successful solo career which predated not only the Disco movement but also the evolution of Hip-Hop. Combined with the striking cut by his shaven head, unique style sunglasses, and fondness for gold jewelry, Hayes was one of the most distinctive figures in music. He is the first African-American composer to be awarded an Academy Award for "Best Original Song." The award was for the motion picture, "Shaft" (1971), which was also the signature song of his career that earned him a Grammy Award the same year.

Singer, Songwriter, Actor and Producer, Issac Hayes was one of the creative forces behind the record label, "Stax Records," a Memphis based label that was influential in the creation of Southern Soul and Memphis Soul music. After making his singing debut in church at the age of 5, Hayes taught himself how to play the piano, organ and saxophone before moving to Memphis, TN.

Hayes began his recording career in the early 1960's, as a session player for various acts, he began playing the saxophone with local house band "The Mar-Keys," which resulted in the beginning of his long association with Stax Records. After playing on several sessions for singer, Otis Redding, Hayes then focused on a solo career, releasing his landmark album titled "Hot Buttered Soul," which was a commercial breakthrough hit record.

In 1967, during the civil rights movement, Hayes was inspired to write a song for African-American pride, writing the song "Soul Man," which was a successful hit single performed by Soul duo, "Sam & Dave." The song was awarded the 1968 Grammy Award along with being honored by "The Rock & Roll Hall of Fame," as one of the "Songs of the Century."

In 1970, Hayes released 2 classic albums, "The Isaac Hayes Movement" and "To Be Continued," he then reached a massive level of commercial success with the double album, "Shaft" (1971), which also served as the soundtrack to the motion picture released of the same name starring Actor, Richard Roundtree.

Not only did the album win Hayes an Academy Award for Best Score, but the single "Theme from Shaft," a masterful blend of prime Funk and pre-rap monologues, it peaked at No. 1 on The Billboard 200 chart, spending a total of 60 weeks on the chart. The album was added to the National Recording Registry by the Library of Congress for being "Culturally and Historically Significant."

Along with being well known for his contributions as a multi-talented career musical artist, Hayes also began an acting career in 1974, starring as the lead role in the two motion pictures, "Truck Turner" and "Tough Guys." His career as an actor would continue for the next three decades as he would star in 71 films and television roles.

Otis Redding

Major Awards   **Wins**

Grammy Awards   2

Major Hall of Fame Inductions

Rock & Roll Hall of Fame
Grammy Lifetime Achievement
Grammy Hall of Fame
R&B Hall of Fame
Georgia Music Hall of Fame
Honored on U.S. Postal Stamp

Otis Redding (1941 - 1967) was known perhaps as the greatest
Soul singer of all time. His magnetic stage presence and sincere
performances made him an instant star. His emotional style and
powerful singing became synonymous with Soul music. Redding's
contributions to the genre has influenced countless musicians, he
is also one of the most sampled artists in history. His signature song
"Sittin' on The Dock of the Bay" which features a whistled tune heard
before the song's fade is credited with influencing the Soul movement
by combining traditional R&B with Folk. His unique mixture of Memphis
Gospel and Soul went on to sell more than one million copies and
brought him into prominence. Rolling Stone Magazine ranked
Redding as No. 8 on its list of the "100 Greatest Vocalists of All Time."

Singer, Songwriter, Producer, Arranger and Talent Scout, known as the "Voice of Soul music," Otis Redding is considered one of the greatest singers in the history of Pop music and a pioneer in the genres of Soul music and R&B. Known for his sincere emotional delivery, Redding's style of singing gained inspiration from Gospel music, which influenced many other Soul artists of the 1960's.

When he was 5 years old, Redding's family moved to Macon, GA., he began his career as a singer and musician in the choir of the Vineville Baptist Church. He grew up listening to the music of singers, Sam Cooke and Little Richard. In the late 1950's, he had the opportunity at the age of 15 to work with Little Richard's band, "The Upsetters."

Redding began a career recording at "Stax Records," playing guitar and arranging his own songs. He was known for his energy in the studio, in 1965, he recorded the album "Otis Blue / Otis Redding Sings Soul in one day," featuring three songs written by Redding: "Ole Man Trouble," "Respect," and "I've Been Loving You Too Long." His groundbreaking single "Sittin' on The Dock of the Bay" is credited with influencing the Soul Movement by combining traditional R&B with Folk.

While influenced by the success and popularity of Marvin Gaye's duets with several female artists, in 1967, Redding also released a successful duet album, "King and Queen," along with singer, Carla Thomas. The popularity of all his albums have grown worldwide, many artists continue to sample, as well as be inspired by his music. Known as the "Queen of Soul," singer, Aretha Franklin remade his popular song, "Respect." Her rendition of his song became an instant hit record and signature song of her career.

The idea that music could be a universal force, bringing people together from different cultures was central to Redding's personal philosophy and reflected in his everyday life. He also set up his own publishing and record label, "Jotis Records," making unprecedented moves for African-American musicians in the 1960's. While it was not Redding's prime motivation, he was seen as a role model by many African-Americans. He was well respected as someone who was compensated for his music without the usual horror stories of being taken advantage of by promoters, agents, managers or record company executives.

31

Diana Ross

Major Awards	Wins
Grammy Awards	2
American Music Awards	8
Golden Globe Award	1
Tony Award	1
NAACP Image Award	1
MTV Music Video Award	1
World Music Award	1
Guinness World Record	1
Presidential Medal of Freedom	1

Major Hall of Fame Inductions

Rock & Roll Hall of Fame
Grammy Lifetime Achievement
Songwriter's Hall of Fame
Soul Train Hall of Fame
Hollywood Walk of Fame

As the lead singer of one of the world's most popular, top-selling female groups, "The Supremes," Diana Ross (1943 -) helped to establish "Motown Records" as a powerhouse label. After pursuing a solo career, she released an array of hits, such hits as "Aint' No Mountain High Enough," "Love Hangover," "Upside Down" and "I'm Coming Out." Along with a legendary career that has spanned over six decades in music, film and television, Ross has inspiring millions worldwide, she has also mapped out the stardom blueprint for future generations of female entertainers across the globe.

Singer, Producer and Actress, Diana Ross rose to fame as the lead singer of the vocal group "The Supremes," during the 1960's they became the most successful group on "Motown Records." During her teenage years, Ross began singing with the trio and eventually formed the groundbreaking group, who later went on to score a monumental 12 No. 1 hits including, "Baby Love," "Come See About Me," "Stop! In the Name of Love," and "Back in My Arms Again."

The Supremes emerged as the best-charting female group in U.S. history, as well as one of the world's best-selling female groups of all time. In 1969, Ross decided to leave the group in order to pursue a solo career, she released her self titled debut album "Diana Ross," featuring the No. 1 hit single "Reach Out and Touch Somebody's Hand," and "Ain't No Mountain High Enough."

In 1972, she branched out into acting, portraying the legendary singer, Billie Holiday in the motion picture "Lady Sings the Blues," her performance garnered her a Golden Globe Award and an Academy Award nomination for "Best Actress." The soundtrack to the film was a huge success and helped spark new interest in Holiday as well. Ross went on to star in the films "Mahogany" (1975), co-starring Billy Dee Williams and Anthony Perkins, and "The Wiz" (1978) co-starring Michael Jackson.

In 1980, her self titled album "Diana" produced another No. 1 hit single, "Upside Down," as well as the international hit "I'm Coming Out." The success of her duet "Endless Love" featuring singer, Lionel Richie helped to launch his solo career. In 1983, Ross gave a legendary benefit concert at "The Great Lawn of New York City's Central Park," which was attended by 800,000 fans from across the globe. The concert raised enough funds for a children's park, later known as the Diana Ross Playground.

In 1993, Guinness World Records declared Ross as the most successful female music artist in history, due to her success in the United States and United Kingdom for having more hits than any female artist in the charts, with a career total of 70 hit singles with her work with The Supremes and as a solo artist. Ross also had a Top-10 hit for 5 consecutive decades, as a performer she broke a new world record of having at least one hit single every year from 1964 to 1996, a period of 32 consecutive years.

Little Richard

Major Awards	Wins
American Music Award	1
NAACP Image Award	1
Rhapsody & Rhythm Award	1
BMI Icon Award	1

Major Hall of Fame Inductions

Rock & Roll Hall of Fame
Grammy Lifetime Achievement
Grammy Hall of Fame
Songwriter's Hall of Fame
R&B Hall of Fame
Blues Hall of Fame
NAACP Hall of Fame
Apollo Theater Hall of Fame
Georgia Music Hall of Fame
Hollywood Walk of Fame

Known as the "Founding Father of Rock & Roll," Musical Icon, Little Richard (1932 - 2020) was a massive influential Rock & Roll pioneer whose early hits inspired a generation of musicians. The pianist/singer was behind legendary hits such as "Tutti Frutti," "Good Golly Miss Molly," and "Long Tall Sally," his songs set the template that many generations of musicians would follow. The screamer/songwriter was nothing America had ever seen. His flamboyant and joyful persona embodied the spirit and sound of a new art form as he broke through several musical barriers.

Singer, Songwriter and Musician who was nicknamed "The Innovator, The Originator, and The Architect of Rock & Roll," Richard Wayne Penniman, better known as, Little Richard was an influential figure in the Pop music culture for over seven decades. Known for his flamboyant performances, Little Richard's hit songs from the mid-1950's were the defining moments in the development of Rock & Roll music genre.

Growing up, Richard's life was largely shaped by the AME Church. Two of his uncles as well as his grandfather were preachers, he was involved with the church as much as anyone in his family, singing Gospel songs and eventually learning to play the piano. In the early 1950's, he began to transition towards recording secular music.

In 1955, Richard teamed up with producer, Art Rupe, who was searching for a frontman to lead a group of musicians, Richard stepped into the recording studio and created "Tutti Frutti," which was an instant Billboard hit. Over the next year and a half, he created several more rock hits, including "Long Tall Sally," "Good Golly Miss Molly" and "Send Me Some Lovin." Richard, then established Rock & Roll as a real musical form and inspired others, most notably "The Beatles," to make a go of it. In addition to his records, Richard also appeared in several early rock films, such as "Don't Knock the Rock" (1956), "The Girl Can't Help It" (1957) and "Mister Rock & Roll" (1957).

As his success soared, Richard, fueled by his earlier connections to the church and saw his doubts about rock music deepen. In 1957, he abruptly and publicly quit performing rock and committed himself to the ministry and recording Gospel songs, he then recorded his debut religious album, "God Is Real," (1959). In 1964, following "The Beatles" recording a rendition of his song "Long Tall Sally," Richard plunged back into rock music, he then went on tour along with Soul singer, Sam Cooke as an opening act.

Richard's charismatic showmanship, innovative vocalizations and uptempo rhythmic music also played a key role in the formation of other popular music genres, including Soul and Funk. He influenced numerous singers and musicians across many musical genres, his music helped shape Rock & Roll and R&B for generations to come.

Johnnie Taylor

Major Awards   **Wins**

Grammy Awards   2
R&B Award   1

Major Hall of Fame Inductions

Blues Hall of Fame
Arkansas Hall of Fame

Johnnie Taylor (1934 - 2000) was a highly acclaimed R&B/Soul singer with distinctive powerful, gritty vocals who became a prolific artist in the late 1960's. Over his legendary career, he performed in a wide variety of genres including Doo-wop, Gospel, Blues, R&B, Soul, Pop, and Disco. Nicknamed the "Philosopher of Soul," Taylor is best remembered for his R&B chart-topping hits, "Who's Making Love" and "Cheaper to Keep Her." His biggest success was his 1976 across the board No. 1 hit "Disco Lady," which became the first single ever to be certified as platinum (which meant at the time record sales were of over 2 million copies). Along with his musical success and career spanning over four decades, Taylor's style had evolved into a hybrid of Soul and Blues.

Singer, Songwriter and Gospel Phenom, known as the "Philosopher of Soul," Johnnie Taylor is one of the most prolific artist in the history of Soul music. Taylor moved to Kansas City, Missouri, at the age of 10 with his grandmother, during his teen years, he sang with a Gospel quartet, "The Melody Kings." They occasionally opened for the famous, highly influential Gospel group, "The Soul Stirrers," whose young lead singer, Sam Cooke, befriended him.

In 1953, Taylor moved to Chicago, Illinois, and began singing with "The Highway QCs," a long-running, popular Gospel quartet in which Cooke and Lou Rawls had previously been members. The QCs made their recording debut in 1955 with Taylor singing lead on "Somewhere to Lay My Head," which made the group a nationwide Gospel attraction.

When Cooke left the Soul Stirrers, Taylor was chosen to be his replacement in 1957. While a member of the group, he became an ordained minister and preached his first sermon at Fellowship Baptist Church in Chicago. Taylor then polished his musical style, which combined Gospel, R&B, and Blues along with his flamboyant appearance. He proceeded to become one of the 1960's top-selling performers, outselling huge stars such as Otis Redding and Carla Thomas.

He had a prolific run on the R&B charts, beginning with "I Had A Dream" (1966) and "Somebody's Sleeping in My Bed" (1967). In 1968, Taylor had his first major crossover Pop and R&B hit in "Who's Making Love," a Funk/Soul song that went to No. 1 on the R&B charts and hit No. 5 on the Pop charts.

The success of "Who's Making Love" enabled Taylor to hire a permanent touring band for the first time in his career, he became a major performer on the "Chitlin' Circuit" all across the South. Subsequent hits included "Take Care of Your Homework" (1969), "Jody's Got Your Girl and Gone" (1971), "I Believe in You (You Believe in Me)" (1972), and "Cheaper to Keep Her" (1973).

Soon after, Taylor became world renown due to his perfected style of smooth, soulful crooning, which incorporated Gospel, Blues, and Soul. His career crossed genres for over four decades and he inspired generations of artists.

The Temptations

Major Awards	Wins
Grammy Awards	4
American Music Award	1
Soul Train Music Award	1

Major Hall of Fame Inductions

Rock & Roll Hall of Fame
Grammy Lifetime Achievement
Grammy Hall of Fame
R&B Hall of Fame
Michigan Legends Hall of Fame
Hollywood Walk of Fame

Known as the "Emperors of Soul," Vocal Group "The Temptations" released a series of successful singles and albums with "Motown Records" during the 1960's and 1970's. They are considered one of the most successful groups in music history. Group members David Ruffin, Melvin Franklin, Paul Williams, Otis Williams and Eddie Kendricks were known for their choreography and distinct harmonies. Having sold tens of millions of albums, The Temptations have inspired countless generations of singers.

Vocal Group, commonly referred to as the "Emperors of Soul," The Temptations are regarded as one of the most successful groups in the history of music. Recording for "Motown Records" they were among the most popular performers of Soul music in the 1960's and 1970's. Noted for their smooth harmonies and intricate choreography, the group's repertoire often included, R&B, Doo-wop, Funk, Disco, Soul, and Adult Contemporary music.

Formed in Detroit, Michigan, in 1960 as "The Elgins," The Temptations initial five-man lineup formed as a merger of two local groups, "The Primes" and "The Distants." The Temptations (David Ruffin, Melvin Franklin, Paul Williams, Otis Williams, Dennis Edwards and Eddie Kendricks) turned out a string of romantic hits, beginning with "The Way You Do the Things You Do" (1964) "My Girl" (1964), "Get Ready" (1966), "Ain't Too Proud to Beg" (1966), and "I Wish It Would Rain" (1967).

Franklin, Williams, Edwards and occasional lead, Paul Williams provided complex harmonies, and the two regular lead singers, Ruffin and Kendricks, strikingly complemented each other. Ruffin had a remarkable sandpaper baritone and Kendricks a soaring tenor. Known for their sleek fashion and athletic choreography, they epitomized sophisticated cool.

The Temptations were the first Motown recording group to win a Grammy Award, in the late 1960's they shifted to a more funk-oriented sound and more socially conscious material. They produced hits such as "Cloud Nine" (1968), "Runaway Child, Running Wild" (1969), and the Grammy Award winning single "Papa Was a Rollin' Stone" (1972).

The Temptations songs have been covered by scores of musicians, from R&B singers such as Luther Vandross (Since I Lost My Baby), to "The Rolling Stones" (Just My Imagination). Their sound has transcended music for over five decades, and continues to inspire future generations.

In 1998, the group's life story premiered as a 4 hour television miniseries, "The Temptations." The popular miniseries won an Emmy Award for "Outstanding Directing." In 2018, their story also served as a Broadway musical "Ain't Too Proud." The show was nominated for 11 Tony Awards and won for the category of "Best Choreography."

Jimi Hendrix

Major Awards	Wins
UK NME Award	1

Major Hall of Fame Inductions

Rock & Roll Hall of Fame
Lifetime Achievement
Grammy Hall of Fame
UK Music Hall of Fame
Hollywood Walk of Fame
Honored on U.S. Postal Stamp

Known as "The Greatest Instrumentalist in the History of Rock Music," Jimi Hendrix (1942 - 1970) altered the course of Pop Music and became one of the most successful and influential musicians of his era. Hendrix applied Blues harmony to rock progressions and played psychedelic rock solos in the middle of Blues classics. He mastered techniques of sound distortion by using a fuzz box that made a light string sound heavy and a heavy string sound like a sledgehammer by overdriving his amplifier. His level of talent was unmatched, he could play the guitar with his teeth, behind his back and under his legs. Hendrix will always be remembered for his rendition of "The Star Spangled Banner" with his guitar while performing at Woodstock in 1969, the concert was referred to as "The Greatest Music Moment of the 1960's."

Rock Guitarist, Singer and Songwriter who is widely regarded as one of the most influential guitarists in history and one of the most celebrated musicians of the 20th century, Jimi Hendrix fused American traditions of Blues, Jazz, Rock, and Soul with techniques of British avant-garde Rock to redefine the electric guitar in his own image.

Hendrix was an instrumentalist who radically redefined the expressive potential of the electric guitar, he was the composer of classic songs ranging from ferocious rockers to delicate, complex ballads.

As a former U.S. Army Paratrooper whose honorable medical discharge exempted him from service in the Vietnam War, Hendrix spent the early 1960's working as a freelance Instrumentalist for a variety of musicians. In addition to playing in his own band, he performed as a backing musician for various Soul, R&B and Blues musicians, including Wilson Pickett, Sam Cooke, Ike & Tina Turner, Jackie Wilson, Little Richard and "The Isley Brothers."

After being discovered in a New York City club for his unorthodox style of playing his guitar at a high volume, Hendrix moved to England to explore new opportunities. He began performing alongside two British musicians, Noel Redding and Mitch Mitchell, they formed the American-British Rock Band "The Jimi Hendrix Experience." Within months, they earned three UK Top-10 hits with the songs "Hey Joe," "Purple Haze" and "The Wind Cries Mary." Hendrix stunned London's clubland with his instrumental virtuosity and extroverted showmanship, members of iconic British groups such as "The Beatles" and "The Rolling Stones" were among his greatest admirers.

Hendrix was the first musician to use stereophonic phasing effects in his recordings. He pioneered the use of the instrument as an electronic sound source. Players before him had experimented with feedback and distortion, but he turned those effects and others into a controlled fluid vocabulary.

In 1969, Hendrix headlined the Woodstock Musical Festival near Bethel, New York. Woodstock is widely regarded as a pivotal moment in Popular music history, he performed before an audience of more than 500,000 people, making the event one of the largest musical concerts in history. Soon after, Hendrix was the world's most recognizable and highest-paid rock musician.

Billie Holiday

Major Hall of Fame Inductions

Rock & Roll Hall of Fame
Lifetime Achievement
Grammy Hall of Fame
Ertegun Jazz Hall of Fame
ASCAP Jazz Hall of Fame National
Women's Hall of Fame
R&B Hall of Fame
Hollywood Walk of Fame
Honored on U.S. Postal Stamp

Known as "Lady Day," Billie Holiday (1915 - 1959) is considered one of the best Jazz vocalists of all time. She rose to prominence in the 1930's with a unique style that reinvented the conventions of modern singing and performing. Ever since her recording debut, her legacy continues to embody what is elegant and cool in contemporary music. Holiday's life and her genre-defining autobiography "Lady Sings the Blues" made her a cultural icon. The expressive, soulful voice which she boldly put forth as a force for good, turned any song she sang into her own. Holiday will always be remembered for her musical masterpieces, songwriting skills, creativity and courageous views on inequality and justice.

Jazz Musician, Singer and Songwriter, nicknamed "Lady Day," Eleanora Fagan, professionally known as Billie Holiday became acquainted with Jazz music at a very early age. Her inspiration to sing came from listening to Jazz legends, Louis Armstrong and Bessie Smith on the radio. As a young teenager in the early 1930's, she began singing in Harlem nightclubs, she adopted the name "Billie Holiday," (a combination of Billie Dove, a popular film star from the 1920's and her fathers surname).

In 1937, Holiday joined bandleader and composer, "Count Basie's Jazz "Orchestra and performed as a band vocalist. Saxophonist, Lester Young nicknamed her "Lady Day" for her sophistication and grace. Although she had no formal training as a singer, her voice was emotional, expressive and displayed a unique phrasing.

Holiday chose the songs she sang and had a hand in the arrangements, choosing to portray her developing persona of a woman unlucky in love. Her tunes included "I Must Have That Man," "Travelin' All Alone," "I Can't Get Started" and "Summertime." She turned all of these songs into masterpieces, considered by many to be her finest recordings. After her tour with Count Basie's group, Holiday then teamed up with the "Artie Shaw Band" and toured the country, this was the first time an African-American woman and a Caucasian Band shared the same stage.

In 1939, She began performing at the New York City nightclub, "Cafe Society," her performances amazed everyone. She was introduced to a poem called "Strange Fruit," a horrific depiction of lynching in the Southern United States. The song was specifically written for Holiday by a New York public school teacher named, Lewis Allen. The song became the hallmark of her concerts, it's considered by scholars to be the first protest song of the civil rights era.

The lyrics were so controversial that her record label wouldn't record it. She then decided to join an independent recording label, "Commodore Records," where she recorded and sang the song as she pleased. "Strange Fruit" immediately became a cultural spark-point and a hit record. In 1972, Holiday's life story was brought to the big screen, the motion picture, "Lady Sings the Blues," starring Singer/Actress, Diana Ross. Her role in the film earned an Academy Award nomination for "Best Actress."

Jackie Wilson

Major Hall of Fame Inductions

Rock & Roll Hall of Fame
Grammy Hall of Fame
R&B Hall of Fame
Hollywood Walk of Fame

Known as "Mr. Excitement" Jackie Wilson (1934 - 1984) was one of the most important figures of Pop music's transition from R&B into Soul. His vocal power was unmatched by many and he was an electrifying on-stage showman. Wilson was a consistent hitmaker from the mid-1950's through the early 1970's, which was a time when the Apollo Theater and the Copacabana were the venues for artists to signal their arrival in the world of celebrity. Wilson played an integral part in crafting America's soundtrack with hit songs like, "Baby Workout," "Your Love Keeps Lifting Me (Higher and Higher)" and "Lonely Teardrops." Wilson was assured his own success while he also helped launch the pioneering "Motown Sound." While in concerts, his appearance could whip crowds into hysteria.

Soul Singer and Performer who earned the nickname "Mr. Excitement" for his ability to wow audiences, Jackie Wilson was a dynamic and powerful performer who successfully crossed over from R&B to Soul music. He was considered a master showman and one of the most dynamic singers and performers in Pop, R&B, and Rock & Roll history. As a teenager, Wilson became a successful Golden Gloves boxer, he later decided to choose music as a different career path for himself after his mother asked him to stop boxing.

His stage presence was like no other, his shows embodied electrifying dance movements that required jumping and twisting, he often relied on his boxing training to provide his fancy footwork on the stage. Wilson was well known on the R&B scene before he went solo in the late 1950's. In 1953 he replaced singer, Clyde McPhatter in the group "The Dominoes," who were one of the top vocal R&B groups of the 1950's. Wilson was the group's lead singer for the next 3 years.

Shortly after Wilson stepped into the solo spotlight, he released first single, "Reet Petite" (from his first album, He's So Fine). The song "Reet Petite" was written by "Motown Records" owner, Berry Gordy, his partner Roquel Davis and Gordy's sister Gwendolyn. The trio composed and produced six additional singles for Wilson, which included "To Be Loved," "I'm Wanderin," "We Have Love," "That's Why I Love You So," "I'll Be Satisfied," and Wilson's 1958 signature song, "Lonely Teardrops," which ranked No. 1 on the R&B charts in the U.S., and established Wilson as an R&B superstar. His single "Lonely Teardrops" sold over one million copies.

Continuing to ride a wave of success, Wilson went on to make the charts over and over again with a variety of hit songs. He landed at the top of the R&B charts with the ballad "Doggin Around," along with his major 1967 hit "Your Love Keeps Lifting Me (Higher and Higher)."

Wilson's stagecraft at his live shows inspired future musical icons such as James Brown and Michael Jackson. His fans cheered as he would glide across the stage only to take a dip down to his knees without missing a note. He would then loosen his tie and take off his jacket without missing a beat. Just when you think things were about to cool off, he would be on his back close to the edge of the stage, as the crowd screamed his name.

Nina Simone

Major Awards   **Wins**

Film Critics Association   1

Major Hall of Fame Inductions

Rock & Roll Hall of Fame
Grammy Hall of Fame

Known as the "High Priestess of Soul," legendary performer, Nina Simone (1933 - 2003) employed a broad range of musical styles including Jazz, Blues, Folk, R&B, Gospel and Pop music in the 1950's and 1960's, later enjoying a career resurgence in the 1980's. Although Simone occasionally composed her own music, she found the most success by recording songs of other singers. Audiences loved her vocal interpretations, and her record label capitalized on the power of her performance by releasing several live albums. She has a timeless treasure collection of musical magic spanning over five decades including classic hits like "Feeling Good," "I Loves You Porgy," "A Single Woman," and "Four Woman." As a staunch civil rights activist, one of the signature singles of her career, "To be Young, Gifted and Black," was considered an anthem of the civil rights movement during the 1960's.

Singer, Songwriter, Arranger and Civil Rights Activist, known as the "High Priestess of Soul," Eunice Kathleen Waymon, professionally known as Nina Simone was one of the most extraordinary artists of the 20th century. She was a musical genius and storyteller who used her remarkable talent to create a legacy of liberation, empowerment, passion and love through her magnificent body of works.

Simone's talent as a musician was evident early on when she began playing the piano at the tender age of 3. Her mother, a Methodist Minister, and her father, a handyman and preacher, couldn't ignore her God-given gift of music. After graduating valedictorian of her high school, Simone's community raised money for a scholarship for her to study at "The Juilliard School" in New York City, she also attended the prestigious "Curtis Institute of Music" in Philadelphia.

In 1957, Simone came to the attention of the record industry, she signed a contract with "Colpix Records" and recorded a multitude of studio and live albums. During the course of her legendary career which spanned over five decades, she recorded over 40 albums. As her reputation grew as an engaging live performer, it wasn't long before she was asked to perform in other countries around the world, including Switzerland, England, Barbados, Liberia and The Netherlands.

Earlier in her career, Simone resided in Mt. Vernon, New York and was next door neighbors with Minister, Malcom X and his wife Betty Shabazz. She also had a close relationship with civil rights activist, Dr. Martin Luther King Jr., and legendary Boxer, Muhammad Ali, which boosted her notoriety and gave her a close proximity to the happenings of the movement.

One of Simone's best friends, Lorraine Hansberry, (Author of the play, "A Raisin in the Sun," and Godmother to Simone's daughter) created the play "To be Young, Gifted and Black." Simone was so moved by its empowering message, she was inspired to adopt the play into a song.

In 2015, Simone's life story was made into a biographical documentary, "What Happened, Miss Simone?" starring actress, Zoe Saldana, which tells her life story. The film was nominated for an Academy Award for "Best Documentary Feature."

B.B. King

Major Awards	Wins
Grammy Awards	15
MTV Music Video Award	1
Presidential Medal of Freedom	1

Major Hall of Fame Inductions

Rock & Roll Hall of Fame
Grammy Lifetime Achievement
Grammy Hall of Fame
Blues Hall of Fame
Hollywood Walk of Fame

Universally hailed as the "King of the Blues," legendary singer, B.B. King (1925 - 2015) was a principal figure in the development of Blues music, he was also one of the greatest electric guitarist of the 20th century. King has been entertaining fans along with his guitar "Lucille" for over six decades. His long succession of hits, including "Woke Up This Morning" (1953), "Every Day I Have the Blues," and "Sweet Sixteen," enhanced his popularity. King had an impressive 74 entries on Billboard's R&B charts, he was one of the few full-fledged Blues artists to score a major Pop hit when his 1970 signature recording, "The Thrill Is Gone" crossed over to mainstream success. Rolling Stone Magazine ranked King as No. 96 on its list of the "100 Greatest Vocalists of All Time."

Singer, Songwriter, Guitarist and Producer, often referred to as the "King ofBlues," Riley B. King, better known as B.B. King began his career singing in the Gospel choir at Elkhorn Baptist Church in Kilmichael, Mississippi. As a teenager, King moved to Memphis, Tennessee. He found work as a disc jockey, earning the nickname "Beale Street Blues Boy," later shortened to "Blues Boy," and finally to "B.B." In the early 1950's, he was a part of the Blues scene on Beale Street.

King then assembled his own band, "The B.B. King Review." One night while performing at a club, a brawl broke out between two men which caused a fire to ignite the building. King evacuated along with the rest of the crowd but went back to retrieve his guitar. He later found out that the two men were fighting over a woman named Lucille. He then named his guitar "Lucille," as a reminder to never fight over women.

King became one of the most important names in R&B music in the 1950's, since then he had a massive list of hits, including "You Upset Me Baby," "You Know I Love You" and his signature recording, "The Thrill Is Gone." King has also worked with other musicians from Rock, Pop and Country music backgrounds.

Along with a career spanning seven decades, King has recorded a total of 59 studio and live albums, he performed with his 13-piece band tirelessly throughout his musical career, appearing on average at more than 300 concerts per year well into his 70's. In 1956, he booked a record-breaking 342 concerts, that same year he founded his own record label, "Blues Boys Kingdom," with its headquarters at Beale Street in Memphis. His relentless touring strengthened his claim to the title of undisputed "King of Blues."

Aside from music, King was also a successful businessman, he opened a chain of restaurants/clubs (B.B. King's Blues Club) which are located in several U.S. cities as well as on popular cruise ships. He offers his patrons a fine dining experience along with live entertainment and performances from some of the biggest names in Blues, Classic Soul and Rock & Roll.

In 2008 the "B.B. King Museum and Delta Interpretive Center" opened in his hometown of Indianola, Mississippi, it includes exhibits dedicated to King's music, his influences, and the history of the Delta region.

Mahalia Jackson

Major Awards   **Wins**

Grammy Awards   3

Major Hall of Fame Inductions

Rock & Roll Hall of Fame
Grammy Lifetime Achievement
Gospel Music Hall of Fame
Louisiana Music Hall of Fame
Hollywood Walk of Fame
Honored on U.S. Postal Stamp

Known as "The Queen of Gospel," Mahalia Jackson (1911 - 1972) is revered as one of the greatest musical figures in U.S. History. She became one of Gospel music's all-time greats, known for her powerful voice that cultivated a global following. President John F. Kennedy requested she sing at his inauguration. Jackson was also an active supporter of the civil rights movement. She sang at the March on Washington in 1963 at the request of her friend, Dr. Martin Luther King, Jr., performing "How I Got Over" and "I Been Buked and I Been Scorned." As a world renown figure, her natural gift of music brought people of different religious and political convictions together to revel in the beauty of the Gospels and to appreciate the warm spirit that underscored the way she lived her life. Throughout her legendary career, Jackson has recorded 30 albums and sold millions of records.

Gospel Singer, Civil Rights Activist, often referred to as the "Queen of Gospel," Mahalia Jackson is one of the most influential Gospel singers of the 20th century. She began singing at the tender age of 4 at Mount Moriah Baptist Church in New Orleans, Louisiana. Although she was raised in a devout Christian family, she found herself influenced by the secular sounds of Blues artists such as, Bessie Smith and Ma Rainey.

After moving to Chicago as a teenager with the aim of studying nursing, Jackson joined the Greater Salem Baptist Church and soon became a member of the "Johnson Gospel Singers." She performed with the group for a number of years. Jackson then began working with a composer who was known as the "Father of Gospel," Thomas A. Dorsey, soon after joining his band, they began performing around the U.S. cultivating audiences.

While she made some recordings in the 1930's, Jackson had major success with the song "Move On Up a Little Higher" (1947), which sold millions of copies and became the highest selling Gospel single in history. She became more in demand, making radio and television appearances along with going on tour. After touring the U.S. extensively, Jackson began a tour abroad in Europe, she was extremely popular in France and Norway. Along with her popularity growing worldwide, she began her own Gospel program on the CBS television network.

In 1958, Jackson began performing with composer, Duke Ellington and his band. They worked together on an album released the same year under titled "Black, Brown and Beige." Their collaboration lead to other classic songs including, "The Power and the Glory" (1960), "Silent Night: Songs for Christmas" (1962) and "Mahalia" (1965). She also pursued a career in acting, appearing in several motion pictures including her groundbreaking performance in the film, "Imitation of Life." Known for her powerful voice, President John F. Kennedy requested she sing at his inauguration.

Jackson was also an active supporter of the civil rights movement. She sang at the March on Washington in 1963 at the request of her friend, Dr. Martin Luther King, Jr. She sang the songs "How I Got Over" and "I Been Buked and I Been Scorned" in front of 250,000 people. Jackson infused Gospel music with a sensuality and freedom it had never experienced before, her artistry rewrote the rules forever.

Chuck Berry

Major Awards

	Wins
Grammy Awards	2
BMI Icon Award	1

Major Hall of Fame Inductions

Rock & Roll Hall of Fame
Grammy Lifetime Achievement
Grammy Hall of Fame
Songwriter's Hall of Fame
Hollywood Walk of Fame
Honored on U.S. Postal Stamp

Known as "The Father of Rock & Roll," Chuck Berry (1926 - 2017) was undeniably one of the most popular and influential figures in R&B and Rock & Roll music in the 1950's, 1960's, and 1970's. Along with his clever lyrics and distinctive sounds, Berry also became one of the most sampled artists in history. In addition to "The Beatles" and "The Rolling Stones, a multitude of significant Pop music performers have recorded Berry's songs. His signature recording "Johnny B. Goode," was the first song by an African-American musician to be sent into the solar system. When the "Voyager 1" space shuttle was sent into outer space in 1977, it carried a gold-plated copper phonograph record that contained musical selections as well as greetings in over 100 different languages, on the chance that aliens may one day discover it. Rolling Stone Magazine ranked Berry as No. 41 on its list of the "100 Greatest Vocalists of All Time."

Singer, Songwriter and Guitarist, who is considered by many as "The Father of Rock & Roll," Chuck Berry is undeniably one of the most influential figures in the history of Rock & Roll. Growing up in St. Louis, Missouri, Berry joined a local band in 1952, "The Sir John's Trio." He revitalized the band and updated their repertoire of Jazz and Pop music.

His band performed at the Cosmopolitan, an upscale nightclub in East St. Louis, which began attracting patrons. In the mid-1950's, Berry began taking road trips to Chicago, (he felt it was the Midwest capital of music) in search of a record contract. Early in 1955, he met the legendary Blues musician, Muddy Waters, who suggested that Berry go meet with "Chess Records." A few weeks later, Berry wrote and recorded a song called "Maybellene" and took it to the executives at Chess, after hearing the song, they immediately offered him a contract.

Within two months, the single "Maybellene" had reached No. 1 on the R&B charts and No. 5 on the Pop charts. The song had a unique blend of a R&B, country guitar licks, a flavor of Chicago Blues and narrative storytelling, many music historians consider "Maybellene" as the first true Rock & Roll song. Berry quickly followed with a number of other unique singles that continued to carve out the new genre of Rock & Roll including, "Roll Over, Beethoven," "Too Much Monkey Business" and "Brown-Eyed Handsome Man," among others.

Berry managed to achieve crossover appeal with Caucasian youths without alienating his African-American fans by mixing Blues and R&B sounds with storytelling that spoke to the universal theme of youths. In the late 1950's, songs such as "Johnny B. Goode," "Sweet Little Sixteen" and "Carol" all managed to hit the Top-10 of the Pop charts, Berry enjoyed achieving equal popularity with youths on both sides of the racial divide.

Berry remains one of the genre's most influential musicians, his pioneering career influenced generations of musicians. An appropriate tribute to his legacy to Rock & Roll came when his song "Johnny B. Goode" was created into a gold-plated copper phonograph record and placed aboard the "Voyager 1" space shuttle and sent into outer space. The goal of the space program was to give distant or future civilizations a chance to acquaint themselves with the culture of planet Earth in the 20th century.

Lena Horne

Major Awards

	Wins
Grammy Awards	2
Tony Award	1
NAACP Spingarn Medal	1
NAACP Image Award	1

Major Hall of Fame Inductions

Rock & Roll Hall of Fame
Grammy Lifetime Achievement
Grammy Hall of Fame
Songwriter's Hall of Fame
NAACP Hall of Fame
Jazz Hall of Fame
Hollywood Walk of Fame
Honored on U.S. Postal Stamp

Singer, Actress and Civil Rights Activist, Lena Horne (1917 -2010) was a pioneer who rose to prominence in the 1940's. She first established herself as an accomplished live singer, who then transitioned into motion pictures. Her legendary career as a recording artist which spanned over seven decades brought her immense popularity and acclaim. Along with being a musical legend, she also appeared in 16 feature films as well as theater and television roles. Horne occasionally performed on Broadway, including in her own Tony Award winning one-woman show, "Lena Horne: The Lady and Her Music." As leader in civil rights movement, she also spoke out against social injustice and raised money for various civil rights causes.

Singer, Dancer, Actress, and Civil Rights Activist, Lena Horne was an early influencer of having a successful career in acting as well as being a recording artist. Growing up in the Bedford Stuyvesant neighborhood of Brooklyn, New York, Horne took dance, singing and acting lessons at the "Anna Jones Dancing School of Brooklyn." In 1934, she began performing at the Cotton Club in Harlem, the 16 year-old Horne secured a lead role in the Cotton Club Parade alongside famed Jazz singer and entertainer, Adelaide Hall.

Horne also made her Broadway debut in the 1934 production "Dance With Your Gods," she joined "Noble Sissle & His Orchestra" as a singer, she then appeared in the Broadway musical revue "Lew Leslie's Blackbirds" (1939). After performing at the Savoy-Plaza Hotel nightclub for several years, in 1943 her career began to transition into superstardom, becoming the highest paid African-American entertainer during that time. As a civil rights activist, Horne was an early member of the NAACP, she performed at rallies across the country and attended the March on Washington in 1963.

Horne championed racial and social justice as she was the first African-American female to sign a long-term contract with "Metro-Goldwyn-Mayer" (MGM). She insisted on not being relegated to roles where she would play a domestic worker (the industry standard for African-American screen performers at the time). She was then featured in a series of successful musicals such as "Panama Hattie," (1942), "Thousands Cheer" (1943) and "Till the Clouds Roll By" (1946) which brought her widespread critical acclaim.

Along with acting full time, Horne also continued her career as a recording artist, releasing her albums, "It's Love" (1955) and "Stormy Weather" (1957) which included the hit singles "Love Me or Leave Me" and "Lena Horne at the Waldorf Astoria." During that time, she had the largest selling albums by a female artist at her record label, "RCA Records."

As a top-selling artist, along with appearing in film, television, and theater, Horne's career has spanned over 70 years. She made a triumphant return to theater in 1981 with her one-woman show "Lena Horne: The Lady and Her Music," which ran for more than 300 performances on Broadway. In 2006, she released her last studio album, "Seasons of a Life."

Nat King Cole

Major Awards	Wins
Grammy Award	1
Golden Globe Award	1

Major Hall of Fame Inductions

Rock & Roll Hall of Fame
Grammy Lifetime Achievement
Grammy Hall of Fame
Songwriter's Hall of Fame
Hollywood Walk of Fame
Honored on U.S. Postal Stamp

Singer, Nat "King" Cole (1919 - 1965) first came into prominence as a leading Jazz pianist. Although an accomplished pianist, he owes most of his popular musical fame to his soft baritone voice, which he used to perform in Big Band and Jazz genres. He was one of the first recording artists to sign with "Capitol Records," and was that company's most dependable talent for many years. Cole also became the first African-American performer to host a television variety show, "The Nat King Cole Show," which aired on ABC. Throughout his career, he has recorded more than 100 hit songs, he maintained his worldwide popularity with signature recordings such as "The Christmas Song," "Mona Lisa" and "Unforgettable." Cole is widely considered one of the most important musical personalities in U.S. history.

Jazz Pianist and Singer, Nathaniel Adams Coles, known professionally as Nat King Cole has been hailed as one of the best and most influential pianists and small-group leaders of the 20th century. Growing up in Chicago, Illinois, his father, Edward Coles, was a Baptist minister. At the tender age of 4, he learned to play the organ from his mother, Perlina Coles, who was the church organist. He began formal lessons at the age of 12, eventually learning not only Jazz and Gospel music but also European classical music as well.

While growing up, Cole would sneak out of the house and hang around outside local Chicago clubs, listening to artists such as Louis Armstrong, Earl Hines and Jimmie Noone. He dropped out of school at the age 15, in order to pursue a music career. Cole joined forces with his brother, Eddie which led to his first professional recording in 1936. He later joined a national tour for the musical revue "Shuffle Along," performing as a pianist.

By the 1950's, Cole emerged as a popular solo performer. He scored numerous hits, with such songs as "Nature Boy," "Mona Lisa," "Too Young" and "Unforgettable." In the studio, Cole got to work with some of the country's top talent, including Louis Armstrong and Ella Fitzgerald, and famous arrangers such as Nelson Riddle.

Cole made television history in 1956 when he became the first African-American performer to host a television variety series. "The Nat King Cole Show" featured many of the leading performers of the day, including Count Basie, Peggy Lee, Sammy Davis Jr. and Tony Bennett. His career success continued with a presence on the big screen, starring in several Hollywood films including in the drama St. Louis Blues, also starring Eartha Kitt and Cab Calloway.

Cole has recorded more than 100 hit songs during his legendary music career, his rendition of "The Christmas Song" has become a holiday classic, many of his other signature songs have been frequently selected for film and television soundtracks. His daughter Natalie Cole also carried on the family profession, becoming a successful singer in her own right. In 1991, she helped her father achieve a posthumous hit. She recorded his hit "Unforgettable" and put their vocals together as a duet.

Harry Belafonte

Major Awards	Wins
Grammy Awards	2
Emmy Award	1
NAACP Image Award	1
Tony Award	1
BET Award	1

Major Hall of Fame Inductions

Rock & Roll Hall of Fame
Grammy Lifetime Achievement
Grammy Hall of Fame
Hollywood Walk of Fame

Renowned Singer and Actor often dubbed as the "King of Calypso," Harry Belafonte (1927 -) popularized the Caribbean musical style with an international audience in the 1950's. His "Calypso," was the first LP record album in history to sell more than one million copies. He also became the first African-American performer to win an Emmy Award. Belafonte was an early supporter of the civil rights movement and one of Dr. Martin Luther King, Jr.'s confidants. Throughout his career, he has been an advocate for political and humanitarian causes, such as the anti-apartheid movement and USA for Africa. Since 1987, he has been a UNICEF Goodwill Ambassador.

Singer, Songwriter, Activist and Actor often referred to as the "King of Calypso," Harry Belafonte was a key figure in the Folk music scene of the 1950's, he is known for popularizing Caribbean Folk songs known as Calypso. Growing up in New York City, he attended George Washington High School before joining the Navy in order to serve during World War II. When he was honorably discharged, he returned to New York and began attending classes in acting at the Dramatic Workshop of "The New School" in New York City.

Many of Belafonte's classmates were future world renowned actors including, Marlon Brando, Bea Arthur and Sidney Poitier. He later received a Tony Award for his role in the Broadway revue, "John Murray Anderson's Almanac." Belafonte started his career in music as a club singer in order to pay for his acting classes. The first time he appeared in front of an audience, he was backed by Charlie Parker's band, which included drummer, Max Roach and trumpeter, Miles Davis, among others.

Belafonte was first a Pop singer, but later he developed a keen interest in Folk music. His first single, which went on to become his signature song in all of his live performances was "Matilda" (1953). He later released his breakthrough album "Calypso" (1956) which became the first LP in the world to sell over one million copies within a year. His "Banana Boat" song, which was featured on the album has one of his signature lyrics "Day-O." The album introduced American audiences to Calypso music and branded Belafonte with the title the "King of Calypso." While primarily known for Calypso, Belafonte has also recorded in many other genres, including Blues and Gospel.

Along with a successful career as a musician and actor, Belafonte was also a lifelong activist and humanitarian. In the early 1950's, he developed a strong relationship with Dr. Martin Luther King, Jr. He worked tirelessly to mobilize artists in support of the civil rights movement. In 1985, he rallied the global artistic community to raise awareness of the famines, wars and droughts plaguing many African Nations. USA for Africa raised more than $60 million along with the "We Are the World" movement. As a longtime anti-apartheid activist, Belafonte hosted former South African President Nelson Mandela on his triumphant visit to the United States. He has also maintained his commitment to service as a UNICEF Goodwill Ambassador.

Louis Armstrong

Major Awards   **Wins**

Grammy Award   1

Major Hall of Fame Inductions

Rock & Roll Hall of Fame
Grammy Lifetime Achievement
Grammy Hall of Fame
Songwriter's Hall of Fame
Louisiana Music Hall of Fame
R&B Hall of Fame
Hollywood Walk of Fame
Honored on U.S. Postal Stamp

Coming to prominence in the 1920's as an inventive cornet and trumpet player, Louis Armstrong (1901 - 1971) was a foundational influence in Jazz, shifting the focus of the music to solo performers. Along with his distinctive gravelly voice, Armstrong was an influential singer, demonstrating great skills as an improviser, bending the lyrics and melody of a song for expressive purposes. He was also greatly skilled at scat singing, or vocalizing using syllables instead of actual lyrics. Renowned for his charismatic stage presence and signature song "What A Wonderful World," Armstrong's influence extends well beyond Jazz music, he is widely regarded as a profound influence in popular music in general.

Trumpeter, Bandleader, Singer and Actor, Louis Armstrong was one of the most influential artists in history of Jazz music. Growing up in New Orleans, Louisiana he earned a reputation as a fine Blues player. As a teenager, Armstrong met one of the greatest cornet players in town, Joe "King" Oliver. He began acting as a mentor to the young Armstrong, showing him pointers on the horn and occasionally offering him a job as a substitute band player. Armstrong's reputation as a musician continued to grow, in 1918, he replaced Oliver in "Kid Ory's Band," which was the most popular band in New Orleans at the time.

Armstrong spent his summers performing on riverboats, where he honed his music reading skills. Although he was content with remaining in New Orleans, in 1922, he received a call from Oliver asking him to relocate to Chicago in order to join his "Creole Jazz Band," Armstrong accepted the offer. He soon built a reputation for himself and took Chicago by storm with his remarkably talent of playing the cornet. He then recorded his first solo, "Chimes Blues."

Armstrong began to record dozens of records, establishing his own band under his own name, "Louis Armstrong and His Hot Five." He collaborated with other legends such as saxophonist, Sidney Bechet and Blues singer, Bessie Smith. From 1925 until 1928, Armstrong recorded more than 60 records, by that time he began playing the trumpet, his technique was superior to that of all competitors.

In 1929, he headed to New York, where he earned a role in a Broadway production of "Connie's Hot Chocolates," featuring the music of "Fats" Waller and Andy Razaf. Due to his love for the stage, Armstrong also pursued a career in acting, he appeared in several motion pictures and television roles. He was mostly featured as a good-humored entertainer. He played a rare dramatic role in the 1947 film, "New Orleans."

More than a great trumpeter, Armstrong made his greatest impact on the evolution of Jazz music, which at the beginning of his career was popularly considered a novelty. Along with his great sensitivity, technique and capacity to express emotion, he not only ensured the survival of Jazz music, but led its development into a fine art. His autobiographies include, "Swing That Music" (1936) and "Satchmo: My Life in New Orleans" (1954).

Candi Staton

Major Awards   **Wins**

R&B Pioneer Award   1

Major Hall of Fame Inductions

Alabama Music Hall of Fame
Christian Music Hall of Fame

Over the course of her legendary career that has spanned for more than five decades, Gospel, Soul and R&B singer, known as "The First Lady of Southern Soul," Candi Staton (1940 -) has been an unstoppable force coming out of the gate in the early 1970's with a string of R&B hit records. Along with a total of 30 albums, Staton has scored a hit record in every decade for over a half century, her style ranged from Gospel, R&B, Disco to Electronic Dance music. Along the way, she has won over generations of fans with her powerhouse voice and timeless chart-topping songs including "Victim," "When "Young Hearts Run Free," You Wake Up Tomorrow" and "You Got the Love." In 1980, she began her move into Gospel music, and has since created her own label and established a long running television series, "New Direction," on the Trinity Broadcasting Network.

Singer and Songwriter, Canzetta Maria Staton, best known as Candi Staton was one of the best-selling artist of the 20th century. Growing up in Hanceville, Alabama, Stanton began singing with a Gospel group at the age of 8, alongside her older sister Maggie Staton and friends Leatha Mae Malcolm and Betty Jean Byers. A few years later, Stanton and her sister had the opportunity to attend the Jewell Christian Academy in Nashville, Tennessee.

While at the Academy, they were paired with Naomi Harrison and formed "The Jewell Gospel Trio." The trio subsequently toured the Gospel circuit in the 1950's along with other talents such as "The Soul Stirrers," "The Staples Singers," Mahalia Jackson, Aretha Franklin and her father, C. L. Franklin. The girls also recorded for record labels between 1953 and 1958 including, "Aladdin, Nashbro, Apollo, and Savoy Records."

In 1968, Staton moved back to Alabama, she was planning to leave Gospel music as a career and instead go to college and become a registered nurse. In 1970, however, she was discovered by Alabama-based R&B performer, Clarence Carter. He took Staton to "Fame Studios" in Muscle Shoals, Alabama and launched the beginning of her career in R&B music with her debut single, "I'd Rather Be an Old Man's Sweetheart (Than a Young Man's Fool)."

She followed up with another hit, "I'm Just a Prisoner (Of Your Good Lovin')" earning her the title, "The First Lady of Southern Soul." By 1974, Staton left Fame Studios for "Warner Brothers Records" and 2 years later recorded "Young Hearts Run Free," which reached No. 1 on the United Kingdom Pop charts. During the 1970's Disco era, Staton ranked as the third most well known Disco Diva in the world after Donna Summer and Gloria Gaynor.

In 1979, she was invited by President Jimmy Carter to the White House to attend the first Black Music Association Dinner. In 1982, Staton founded Beracah Ministries, she reemerged at the age of 42 as a Gospel singer and Christian television personality. Over the next two decades she recorded 8 Gospel albums. In the late 1990's she released a self-titled compilation of her 1960's and 1970's material, which led to the subsequent release of a new R&B album titled "His Hands."

Earth, Wind & Fire

Major Awards	Wins
Grammy Awards	6
American Music Awards	5
NAACP Image Award	1
Soul Train Music Award	1
BET Award	1

Major Hall of Fame Inductions

Rock & Roll Hall of Fame
Grammy Lifetime Achievement
Grammy Hall of Fame
Vocal Group Hall of Fame
Hollywood Walk of Fame

Earth, Wind & Fire were one of the most musically accomplished, critically acclaimed, and commercially popular Funk bands of 1970's. Conceived by Drummer, Bandleader, Songwriter and occasional Vocalist, Maurice White, the group's all-around musical vision used Funk as its foundation, but also incorporated Jazz, Smooth Soul, Gospel, Pop, Blues, African music and Disco. For over four decades, Earth, Wind & Fire's irresistibly bouncy dance anthems, including songs like "Getaway," "Fantasy," "Lets Grove," "Shining Star" and "September" have all rocked countless celebrations and parties all across the globe. They have been described as one of the greatest bands ever. Earth, Wind & Fire was also the first African-American band to be inducted into the Kennedy Center Honors.

Rock Band, that has spanned the musical genres of R&B, Soul, Funk, Jazz, Earth, Wind & Fire was one of the best-selling and most influential groups of the 1970's. The principal members were Maurice White, Philip Bailey, Verdine White, Fred White, Al McKay, Johnny Graham, Ralph Johnson, Larry Dunn, and Andrew Woolfolk.

Earth, Wind & Fire was the brainchild of Maurice White, a drummer raised in Memphis, Tennessee, who moved to Chicago and became a veteran session player at "Chess Records" and a member of "The Ramsey Lewis Trio." He drew upon a wide variety of influences, including his Memphis church-singing roots and his broad recording duties at Chess.

In 1971, the group began recording 2 albums for "Warner Brothers Records." While on tour in Denver, Colorado, the group shared an event with a local act that featured vocalist, Bailey, keyboardist, Dunn, and saxophonist, Woolfolk, all of whom soon after joined a recreated Earth, Wind & Fire, which developed a broader musical range encompassing Funk, Soul, and Pop.

The group switched labels, and their second album for "Columbia Records," "Head to the Sky" (1973), sold a half-million copies, setting the stage for the huge success that followed. Their next single, "That's the Way of the World" (1975), lifted Earth, Wind & Fire to superstardom, yielding the hit singles "Shining Star" and "Reasons." Their phenomenal string of 11 consecutive gold albums, eight of which also attained platinum status, included "Gratitude "(1975), "Spirit" (1976), "All 'n' All" (1977), "The Best of Earth, Wind & Fire" (1978), and "Raise" (1981).

Part of the bands appeal was its remarkable versatility, as it delivered soulful ballads and spiritual anthems, driving Funk and Rock, and upbeat Disco dance hits, their songs offered uplifting poetic lyrics with romantic and playful themes.

The group was known for spectacular concerts that featured enormous stage props, elaborate costumes and grand illusions. The multi-talented White and Bailey led an ensemble that often reached 15 players onstage. White's affection for Egyptology and use of African instruments such as the "kalimba" (thumb piano) further embellished the group's unique image.

Teddy Pendergrass

Major Awards	Wins
American Music Award	1

Major Hall of Fame Inductions

Vocal Group Hall of Fame

Teddy Pendergrass (1950 - 2010) was a R&B singer who embodied the smooth "Philly Soul" sound of the 1970's as lead vocalist for the group "Harold Melvin and the Blue Notes," before embarking on a successful solo career. After launching his solo career, he released 5 consecutive platinum albums, which was a record at the time for an African-American R&B artist. Pendergrass had a huge appeal to women of all races, which led to worldwide tours in which he played to all-female audiences. He had a massive level of success with hit songs such as, "Love TKO," "Close The Door," "When Somebody Loves You Back," "Turn of the Lights" and "Wake up Everybody." Pendergrass continues to inspire generations of musicians with his soulful, sultry and romantic style.

R&B Singer, Theodore DeReese Pendergrass, better known as Teddy Pendergrass began his career singing Gospel music in a Philadelphia church as well as an elementary school choir, he also became an ordained minister at the age of 10. Pendergrass started a teen Pop vocal group when he was 15 years old, while also teaching himself how to play the drums. By his late teens, he was a drummer for local vocal group "The Cadillacs."

In the late 1960's, The Cadillacs merged with another more established group, "Harold Melvin & the Blue Notes." In 1970, when the Blue Notes broke up, Melvin, now aware of Pendergrass vocal powers, asked him to take the lead singer spot. Despite the revised billing of the group, Pendergrass felt that he wasn't getting enough recognition. In 1976, he decided to separate from the Blue Notes in order to pursue a solo career.

He burst back on the scene, with his self titled album "Teddy Pendergrass" (1977), a platinum solo debut which included hit singles "I Don't Love You Anymore," "You Can't Hide from Yourself" and "The More I Get the More I Want." Around this time, he began to institute his infamous "Ladies Only" concerts. As a solo artist, Pendergrass became the first African-American male singer to record 5 consecutive multi-platinum albums, his next 4 albums were "Life Is a Song Worth Singing" (1978), "Teddy" (1979), "Teddy Live! Coast to Coast" (1980) and "TP" (1980).

Pendergrass continued to perform and record into the 1980's as he kept racking up the hits with the singles "Turn Off the Lights," "Come Go with Me," "Shout and Scream," "Love TKO" and "I Can't Live Without Your Love." During the height of his career, in 1982 he was involved in a devastating car accident on Philadelphia's Lincoln Drive. He lost control of his car and hit a guard rail and two trees. Pendergrass and his passenger were rescued from the wreckage, but severely injured.

After a few years of extensive physical therapy, Pendergrass returned to the studio and released the album, "Love Language" (1984), which included an appearance by then-newcomer, Whitney Houston in the song "Hold Me," followed by hit songs such as "Joy" (1988) and "It Should've Been You" (1991) which reached the top of the Billboard R&B charts.

Bessie Smith

Major Hall of Fame Inductions

Rock & Roll Hall of Fame
Grammy Lifetime Achievement
Grammy Hall of Fame
Blues Hall of Fame
Honored on U.S. Postal Stamp

Crowned as "The Empress of the Blues," Bessie Smith (1834 - 1937) earned the honor as the greatest classic Blues singer of the 1920's and 1930's. Due to her early stage experience, Smith's repertoire was extensive by the time she made her first record in 1923. She primarily specialized in Blues numbers, singing far more than any female vocalist of her day. She also performed Country Blues and Jazz tunes in shows that completely captivated her audiences. Her recording debut "Downhearted Blues" was an immediate hit when it was released in 1923, selling more than one million copies that year.

Jazz and Blues Vocalist, known as "The Empress of Blues," Bessie Smith is regarded as one of the greatest singers of the early 20th century and an early influencer of Blues music. Smith made her first public appearance as a singer at the tender age of 8, performing at the Ivory Theatre in her hometown of Chattanooga, Tennessee.

In 1912, she began performing as a dancer in the "Moses Stokes Minstrel Show," soon thereafter in the "Rabbit Foot Minstrels," of which Blues vocalist, Ma Rainey was a member. Rainey (who was one of the first great Blues singers from whom Smith received her musical apprenticeship) took Smith under her wing. Over the next decade, Smith continued to perform at various theaters while on the "Vaudeville Circuit" in 1913, Smith began touring the country along with Rainey.

For several years, Smith traveled throughout the South, singing in tent shows, bars and theaters in cities such as Birmingham, Memphis, Atlanta and Savannah. In 1920, she made Philadelphia her new home, which was the first city where she was heard by Clarence Williams, a representative of "Columbia Records." Along with her rich, powerful voice, Smith propelled into the Blues spotlight. In 1923, she made her first recording, "Down Hearted Blues," which became an enormous success, selling more than one million copies.

Throughout her career, Smith has recorded more than 160 songs, her musical collaborations outside of her solo career were with some of the greatest musicians in the history of Jazz music, including Louis Armstrong, Fletcher Henderson and Benny Goodman. Her most notable songs included "Backwater Blues," "Tain't Nobody's Biz-ness If I Do," "Empty Bed Blues," and "Nobody Knows You When You're Down and Out." By the end of the 1920's, Smith was the highest paid African-American performer in the country, earning the title "The Empress of the Blues."

Over the last century, Smith's music continues to win over new fans, the collections of her songs continue to sell extremely well. She has influenced countless female vocalists, including Billie Holliday and Aretha Franklin. The film, "Bessie," starring actress, Queen Latifah who portrayed Smith along with actress, Mo'Nique who portrayed Rainey was released in 2015, tells Smith's life story. The film garnered four Primetime Emmy Awards.

The Four Tops

Major Hall of Fame Inductions

Rock & Roll Hall of Fame
Grammy Lifetime Achievement
Grammy Hall of Fame
R&B Music Hall of Fame
Vocal Group Hall of Fame
Hollywood Walk of Fame

Vocal R&B, Soul, Disco and Doo-wop Quartet, "The Four Tops" began their careers together as high school students in Detroit, Michigan, in the early 1950's. Group members, Levi Stubbs, Abdul "Duke" Fakir, Renaldo "Obie" Benson and Lawrence Payton contributed to the massive success of "Motown Records" in the 1960's with hit records including, "I Can't Help Myself (Sugar Pie Honey Bunch)" "Reach Out (I'll Be There)" "It's The Same Old Song" and "Baby I Need Your loving." Over the course of four decades, the group remained together, having gone from 1953 until 1997 without a single change in personnel. Rolling Stone Magazine ranked The Four Tops as No. 79 on its list of the "100 Greatest Artists of All Time."

Vocal Quartet, who has contributed to the musical genres of R&B, Soul, Disco, Doo-wop and Jazz, The Four Tops were instrumental in defining "Motown Records" distinct sound during the 1960's and 1970's. Composed of singers, Levi Stubbs, Abdul "Duke" Fakir, Renaldo "Obie" Benson and Lawrence Payton, who all met while attending high school in Detroit, Michigan.

In 1963, the Four Tops were signed to "Motown Records" by label owner, Berry Gordy. They were among a number of groups, including "The Miracles," "The Marvelettes," "Martha and the Vandellas," "The Temptations," and "The Supremes," who all established the "Motown Sound" that was heard around the world during the 1960's. Under the direction of Motown's top production and recording team, in 1964 they released the song, "Baby I Need Your Loving," which debuted at No. 1 on the Pop charts.

In 1965, they released "Ask the Lonely" and their first crossover hit, "I Can't Help Myself" which hit No. 1 on both the Pop and R&B charts. The next year, they released "Shake Me, Wake Me (When It's Over)" and their second crossover hit, "Reach Out (I'll Be There)," which reached No. 1 on the Pop and R&B charts and remained for nearly 4 months. Over the next 8 years The Four Tops appeared on the charts over 30 times.

The Four Tops became popular in major nightclubs around the world, similar to virtually all of Motown's top acts. The group sought longevity and stability while building their careers equally on live appearances and records. As one of Motown's most consistent hitmakers, they have the longest lived lineup of over 40 years without a single change in personnel.

In addition to all of the success with their own albums, in 1970, a collaborative album combining Motown's premier vocal groups, The Four Tops and The Supremes joined together for a series of albums billed under the joint titles, "The Magnificent 7" and "The Return of the Magnificent 7," were both major hit records in the United States and the United Kingdom.

During the 1980's the Four Tops released another hit, "When She Was My Girl" which reached No. 1 on the R&B charts, they continued to tour playing over 100 shows each year while also appearing on Broadway in New York.

Duke Ellington

Major Awards	Wins
Grammy Awards	11
NAACP Spingarn Medal	1
Legion of Honor by France	1
Pulitzer Prize for Music	1
Honorary PhD Berklee College	1
German Film Award	1
Presidential Medal of Freedom	1

Major Hall of Fame Inductions

Rock & Roll Hall of Fame
Grammy Lifetime Achievement
Grammy Hall of Fame
Songwriter's Hall of Fame
Oklahoma Jazz Hall of Fame
Hollywood Walk of Fame
Honored on U.S. Postal Stamp
Commemorated on U.S. Quarter

As a major figure in the history of Jazz music, Duke Ellington's (1899 - 1974) career spanned more than half a century, during which he composed thousands of songs for the stage, screen and contemporary songbook, it was Ellington's sense of musical drama that made him stand out. His blend of melodies, rhythms and subtle sonic movements gave audiences a new experience. He was one of the most creative forces in Jazz music in the 20th century. In 1999, he was also posthumously awarded the Pulitzer Prize for music, commemorating the centennial year of his birth.

Composer, Pianist and Leader of a Jazz Orchestra, Edward Kennedy Ellington, better known as Duke Ellington was one of the most prominent figures in the history of Jazz music, his music stretched into various other genres, including Blues, Gospel, Popular Classical and film scores. He began piano lessons at the age of 7, and writing music by his teens. He dropped out of high school in his junior year in order to pursue a career in music.

In his hometown of the Washington, D.C., he joined a local talented band called the "Washingtonians," a five-piece group who were well known and traveled throughout the South. In 1923, Ellington moved to New York City and he became the leader of his own band, soon after they began recording. In 1927, his band was hired to play regularly at the "Cotton Club" in Harlem, where they had an extended residency for 5 years. Their performances were broadcasted nightly throughout the city. By 1930, Ellington was beginning to be recognized as serious composer.

While in New York, Ellington was the most sought after composer, he performed in many Broadway nightclubs as the bandleader and his band had grown into a ten-piece ensemble. His band also toured the globe, frequently performing in Asia, West Africa, South America, Australia and most of North America. Despite this grueling schedule, most of Ellington's musicians stayed with him for decades, including saxophonist, Harry Carney, who was a band member for 47 years. During his legendary career, Ellington wrote more than 1000 compositions, his extensive body of work appeared in many motion pictures and on the radio.

In 2009, the United States Mint issued a coin featuring Ellington appearing on it, making him the first African-American to appear by himself on a circulating U.S. coin. The quarter he was featured on was released into circulation representing Ellington's birthplace of the District of Columbia. He is depicted on the quarter seated at a piano, sheet music in hand, along with the inscription "Justice for All," which is the District of Columbia's motto. In 1986, he was also commemorated on the U.S postage stamp.

Ellington's signature song was "Take the A Train," (the "A" referring to a popular subway line in New York City) has become one of the most recognized Jazz songs ever recorded. He also wrote a series of songs that became standards, including, "Sepia Panorama," "It Don't Mean a Thing (If It Ain't Got That Swing)," "Cotton Tail," "Mood Indigo," "Sophisticated Lady," "Solitude" and "In A Sentimental Mood."

Ashford & Simpson

Major Awards   **Wins**

Grammy Trustee Award   1
R&B Pioneer Award   1
ASCAP Founders Award   1

Major Hall of Fame Inductions

Songwriter's Hall of Fame

Husband and wife songwriting production team and recording duo, Nickolas Ashford (1941 - 2011) and Valerie Simpson (1946 -) had two careers, as songwriter's and performers, which began in the 1960's. They had a major influence over Motown songs in the 1970's and 1980's, writing the majority of the material recorded by Marvin Gaye and Tammi Terrell, including "Ain't No Mountain High Enough," "You're All I Need To Get By" and "Ain't Nothing Like the Real Thing." Ashford & Simpson's songs were also recorded by the likes of Ray Charles, Diana Ross, Gladys Knight and Smokey Robinson. The duo also had a number of hits as performers themselves on the R&B charts, most notably "Solid," "Love Don't Make It Right," and "It Seems To Hang On."

74

Singer and Songwriting, husband and wife duo, Nickolas Ashford and Valerie Simpson who are known professionally as Ashford & Simpson both pursued a professional singing career at a young age. Growing up in Michigan, Ashford dropped out of college and headed to New York hoping to make it as a singer or dancer. In an effort to satisfy his musical appetite, he began attending Harlem's White Rock Baptist Church where he met Simpson, a member of the choir and a recent high school graduate who, like Ashford, had strong musical aspirations.

They began working as a duo and writing songs together, their first attempt into the music world proved successful. They released their first single, "I'll Find You," under the group name, "Valerie & Nick," it garnered the attention of legendary singer, Ray Charles. They began working closely with Charles, he was so impressed with their talent, he started recording versions of other Ashford & Simpson's songs, such as "Let's Go Get Stoned" and "I Don't Need No Doctor." The encounter with Charles is what led record labels to take note of the duo's songwriting skills and expertise.

Ashford & Simpson were then hired by "Motown Records" owner, Berry Gordy. This move to Motown established the duo as a formidable force of songwriting talent. They scored hits with songs like "Ain't Nothing Like the Real Thing," "You're All I Need to Get By" and "Precious Love," all recorded by Marvin Gaye and Tammi Terrell, performers who the duo became a paramount in writing for.

While building an excellent reputation with Motown by writing for Gaye and Terrell, Ashford & Simpson also began making headway with other groups. They wrote the song "Who's Gonna Take the Blame" for Smokey Robinson & The Miracles," they also penned "Didn't You Know You'd Have to Cry" for Gladys Knight & The Pips.

Ashford & Simpson also worked closely with singer Diana Ross. Once Ross left "The Supremes" in order to pursue a solo career, she frequently relied on their writing ability. They wrote her hit song "Reach Out and Touch Somebody's Hand." The duo also had a number of hits as performers themselves, scoring songs such as, "Solid," "Love Don't Make It Right," "Outta the World," and "Babies." They were both trendsetters, their music has inspired countless musicians for over five decades.

Nancy Wilson

Major Awards	Wins
Grammy Awards	3
NEA Jazz Masters Award	1
NAACP Image Awards	2
UNCF Trumpet Award	1

Major Hall of Fame Inductions

Jazz Hall of Fame
Big Band Hall of Fame
Hollywood Walk of Fame

Nancy Wilson (1937 - 2018) was among Contemporary music's most stylish and sultry vocalists, known as "Sweet Nancy," "The Baby," "Fancy Ms. Nancy" and "The Girl With the Honey-Coated Voice," her flexible approach to singing provided a bridge between sophisticated Jazz-Pop vocalists of the 1950's and the powerhouse Pop-Soul singers of the 1960's and 1970's. She also became one of the few African-Americans of her day to host a Television program, the Emmy Award winning "Nancy Wilson Show," on NBC. As a hardworking and highly efficient singer, Wilson has released more than 70 albums over her legendary recording career that has spanned over six decades. Her lifelong work as an advocate of civil rights included participating in the Selma to Montgomery, Alabama., protest march in 1965, as well as receiving an award from the Dr. Martin Luther King Jr. Center for Nonviolent Social Change in Atlanta, Georgia.

World Renowned Jazz Singer, Actress, and Legendary Entertainer, Nancy Wilson transcended Jazz music in the 1950's, she also produced hits in several genres, including R&B, Soul, Pop and Blues. Growing up in Columbus, Ohio, Wilson was an avid singer from the age of 4, by the age of 10, she was the lead singer in the local church choir. As a teenager, she was heavily influenced by singers Dinah Washington and Lena Horne.

Wilson spent one year at Central State College in Ohio before dropping out to pursue a full time music career. She honed her skills by touring continuously in the Midwest and Canada with Rusty Bryant's "Carolyn Club Big Band," along with cutting her first recordings for "Dot Records." After 7 years of touring she felt ready to relocate to New York in order to advance her career.

In 1959, Wilson arrived in New York, she auditioned and signed to "Capitol Records," the home of singers like Nat King Cole and Peggy Lee. In 1960, she released her debut album "Like in Love," which was shortly followed by her next album that was a collaboration, "Nancy Wilson and Cannonball Adderley," which propelled her to national prominence with the hit R&B song, "Save Your Love For Me." Over the next decade, Wilson worked tirelessly in the studio, releasing an average of 2 to 3 albums each year and logging dozens of hit singles on the Billboard Hot 100 Charts. During the course of her legendary career, she has released more than 70 albums.

By the mid-1960's, Wilson was one of her label's best-selling artist, she was a performer who included Jazz-styled Pop in her repertoire and proudly displayed her glamorous good looks, she surpassed established entertainers such as "The Beatles" and "The Beach Boys" in sales. Her rise in popularity showed no sign of slowing down. In addition to enjoying stardom in the United States, she also established a significant fanbase overseas, especially in Japan, where she would remain a favorite for years.

As a result of her recognized depth and diverse talent, Wilson saw other opportunities within the entertainment industry arise. From the mid-1960's and 1970's, she headlined shows in Las Vegas that were booked 2 years in advance. After appearing in numerous television guest roles, Wilson also earned her own television series on NBC, "The Nancy Wilson Show" which won an Emmy Award in 1968.

Fats Domino

Major Hall of Fame Inductions

Rock & Roll Hall of Fame
Grammy Lifetime Achievement
Grammy Hall of Fame
R&B Hall of Fame
Songwriter's Hall of Fame
National Medal of Arts
Hollywood Walk of Fame

Singer and Pianist, Fats Domino (1928 - 2017) became one of the first Rock & Roll stars who helped define the "New Orleans Sound." He first attracted national attention with his record "The Fat Man" (1949), this song is an early Rock & Roll recording that featured a rolling piano and Domino vocalizing over a strong back beat. It sold over one million copies and is widely regarded as the first Rock & Roll record to do so. His signature recording "Blueberry Hill" (1956), was his most popular recording and one of several Rock & Roll adaptations of standard songs. All together his recordings of the 1950's and 1960's sold more than 65 million copies, making him one of the most successful performers of the early Rock & Roll era.

Pianist, Singer and Songwriter, Antoine Domino Jr., better know as Fats Domino was one of the pioneers of Rock & Roll music in the 1950's. Growing up in New Orleans, Louisiana, he followed the musical lead of his father who was a violinist, and an uncle who was played the trumpet. All of the instruments he learned to play were almost entirely self-taught. Domino dropped out of school at the age of 14 and began working as a musician. Learning songs from jukeboxes, he began playing at local bars and nightclubs.

A few years later, he joined a local band that was led by bass player, Billy Diamond, after joining the band, Diamond gave him the nickname "Fats." The band frequently performed at "The Hideaway," a local music spot, Domino soon became the bands frontman and a local draw. In 1949, songwriter, Dave Bartholomew saw him perform and was very impressed. He then invited record label executive, Lew Chudd to witness Domino's performance at The Hideaway the very next night. Chudd immediately signed Domino to his label, "Imperial Records."

Domino and Bartholomew formed a songwriting partnership which proved to be one of the most successful in the early years of the Rock & Roll era. Together they created a sound with new musical accents and memorable Rock & Roll hit songs. Their first collaboration was "The Fat Man" (1949), followed by several other distinctive and memorable collaborations including, "Blueberry Hill," "I'm Walking," "All by Myself," "Walking to New Orleans" and "Whole Lotta Loving."

Domino continued songwriting, this time on his own, without benefit of a collaborator. His first major crossover recording was "Ain't That a Shame," which later opened the doors to a movie career, he appeared in two motion pictures released in 1956, "Shake, Rattle & Rock" and "The Girl Can't Help It."

Throughout his career, Domino has landed 37 songs on the Billboard Charts, along with more than 20 gold records. He is credited with creating Rock & Roll music years before the phrase and genre was invented, helping to popularize the new sound with mainstream audiences. Domino was also a major influence over several future Rock & Roll legends including, "The Beatles," and "The Rolling Stones."

Lionel Richie

Major Awards   **Wins**

Grammy Awards   4
Academy Award   1
American Music Awards   9
Golden Globe Award   1
NAACP Image Award   1

Major Hall of Fame Inductions

Songwriter's Hall of Fame
Apollo Legends Hall of Fame
Alabama Music Hall of Fame
BET Lifetime Achievement
Postage Stamp Honor - Grenada

As a founding member of one of the most successful R&B groups of the 1970's, "The Commodores," singer/songwriter known for creating massive hit records, Lionel Richie (1949 -) achieved monumental success after launching his own solo career in 1982. Richie became one of the most successful male solo artists during the 1980's, he dominated the Pop charts during that period with an incredible run of 13 consecutive Top-10 hits, 5 of them were No. 1. As his popularity skyrocketed, he moved further away from his R&B origins and concentrated more on adult contemporary balladry, which had been one of his strengths even as part of the Commodores. Over the course of his legendary career that spanned more than four decades, Richie has sold over 100 million records worldwide, making him one of the world's best-selling artists of all time.

Singer, Songwriter, and Producer, Lionel Richie was one of the most successful R&B singers of the 1980's. Growing up in Tuskegee, Alabama, Richie was raised around the campus of Tuskegee Institute, his family lived across the street from the home of the President of the University. As a star tennis player in high school, he accepted a tennis scholarship at Tuskegee Institute and later graduated with a major in economics.

As a college student in Tuskegee, Richie formed the R&B group "The Commodores," he became their lead singer and saxophonist. In 1969, the group signed a recording contract with "Motown Records" initially as a support act to The Jackson 5. The Commodores then became established as a popular Soul group. Their first several albums had a danceable, funky sound, as in such tracks as "Machine Gun" and "Brick House." Over time, Richie wrote and sang more romantic, easy-listening songs such as "Easy," "Three Times a Lady," "Zoom" and "Sail On."

By the late 1970's, Richie began writing songs for other artists, he composed the song "Lady" for country musician, Kenny Rogers, which hit No. 1 in 1980. His wide-ranging musical talent also led to collaborations with other artists, including a duet with singer, Diana Ross for the movie theme song titled, "Endless Love" (recorded for the motion picture of the same title). The single became the most successful song in Motown history, topping the charts for 9 consecutive weeks. The songs success encouraged Richie to branch out into and embark on a solo career in 1982.

He immediately began recording his solo debut for Motown titled simply, "Lionel Richie." The album was released in late 1982, and was an immediate smash hit, topping the charts with sales of over 4 million copies worldwide. His second solo album, "Can't Slow Down," made him a superstar, featuring 5 Top-10 singles, including two that reached No. 1 which were "All Night Long (All Night)" and "Hello." The album sold over 20 million copies, and is Richie's best-selling album of all time.

In 1985, Richie also co-wrote the song "We Are the World" along with Pop icon, Michael Jackson to raise money for an African famine relief, the song generated some $50 million in donations and received a Grammy Award for song of the year.

Ethel Waters

Major Hall of Fame Inductions

Grammy Hall of Fame
Gospel Music Hall of Fame
Christian Music Hall of Fame
Hollywood Walk of Fame
Honored on U.S. Postal Stamp

Singer and Actress, Ethel Waters (1896 - 1977) began her career in the 1920's as a Blues singer. She later became the first African-American singer to appear on television, as well as the first to star in her own network show, "The Ethel Waters Show." Throughout her career in film, theater and television, Waters was the second African-American (after Actress, Hattie McDaniel) to be nominated for an Academy Award. She was also the first African-American woman to be nominated for an Emmy Award in 1962. Considered as one of the great Blues singers of her time, Waters performed and recorded with Jazz legends such as Duke Ellington and Benny Goodman. Due to her powerful voice, several composers specifically wrote songs especially for her.

Singer and Actress, Ethel Waters is revered as one of the most influential and celebrated Jazz and Blues singers of the early 20th century. Growing up Pennsylvania, she began working as a house keeper at a Philadelphia hotel at the age of 13. On her 17th birthday (Halloween night), Waters attended a costume party at a nightclub on Juniper Street. She was persuaded to sing two songs on stage, she impressed the audience so much that she was offered a job opportunity to sing at the Lincoln Theatre in Baltimore, Maryland. Billing herself as "Sweet Mama Stringbean," Waters began singing professionally.

Her professional rise was rapid, she moved to New York City to join the dynamic explosion of African-American creativity that was "The Harlem Renaissance." In 1925, she appeared at the "Plantation Club" in Harlem, her spectacular onstage performance led her career to Broadway. In 1927, Waters appeared in the revue of the stage play "Africana," thereafter she began dividing her time between the stage, nightclubs and eventually motion pictures. Waters became the highest paid performer on Broadway, she was the also the first African-American woman to integrate Broadway's theater district.

After appearing in several Broadway revues, Waters was able to remake herself as an actress. In the 1930's, she garnered several non-singing dramatic roles on both stage and screen. Her acting career would eventually eclipse her accomplishments as a singer in the public eye. In 1933, she appeared in the motion picture, "Rufus Jones for President," which featured the child performer and future singer, Sammy Davis Jr., as Rufus Jones. In 1939, Waters also became the first African-American to star in her own television show, "The Ethel Waters Show," a variety special, that appeared on NBC.

In 1949, Waters landed a role in the groundbreaking motion picture, "Pinky," a feature film in which she was nominated for an Academy Award for "Best Supporting Actress." In 1962, she was also nominated for a Primetime Emmy Award for her role in the television series "Route 66." Waters transcended the boundaries of music and acting, countless young hopefuls emulated her sophisticated vocal style. Her legacy continues to live on in the work of outstanding successors including singers, Lena Horne, Billie Holiday and Ella Fitzgerald.

Lou Rawls

Major Awards   **Wins**

Major Awards	Wins
Grammy Awards	3
American Music Awards	2

Major Hall of Fame Inductions

Rock & Roll Hall of Fame
Hollywood Walk of Fame

Known for his smooth, deep voice, which he used to explore many musical genres, including Gospel, Jazz, R&B, Soul, and Pop, singer, Lou Rawls (1933 - 2006) scored a number of hit records throughout the 1960's and 1970's. His voice is as distinctive and instantly recognizable as any in music. Epitomizing cool, class and soul, Rawls humanitarian efforts have also won him several honors, including a street named after him in Chicago, (Lou Rawls Drive). Although Rawls did not attend college, he recognized the importance of higher education. Through his tireless efforts, he has raised more than $250 million and has helped more than 65,000 students obtain higher education with his telethons. Throughout his career, Rawls has released over 70 albums and has sold more than 40 million records worldwide.

Singer, Songwriter, Actor and Producer, Lou Rawls was a world renowned artist known for his signature luxurious baritone singing voice and four-octave vocal range. Born and raised in the south side of Chicago, Illinois. Rawls was raised by his grandmother and began singing in his church choir at the age of 7. As a teenager Rawls formed a Gospel harmony group called the "Teenage Kings of Harmony" along with his childhood friend (and future famed singer) Sam Cooke. In the very beginning of his career, he was involved in a devastating car accident.

Upon recovery, Rawls began singing secular music, his talents also extended into an acting career, which became a second love. He has appeared as a series regular, guest star and host in television shows as well as motion pictures. He has also ventured into the feature film arena, taking on lead roles in independent films as well as smaller parts in movies such as Oscar winning "Leaving Las Vegas" and "Blues Brothers 2000." In 1999, he appeared on Broadway for a role in "Smokey Joes Cafe."

In 1962, he released his first album, "I'd Rather Drink Muddy Water." Rawls became known for doing spoken monologues (raps) during his live performances in which he reflected on his life and social issues. In 1966, he released his first gold album, "Live!," and the album "Soulin," which earned Rawls the reputation of one of the most talented singers during his era.

His Soulin album generated his first major hit, "Love Is A Hurtin' Thing," which reached No. 1 on the R&B chart. In 1976, he released his most successful album, "All Things In Time," which quickly reached the R&B Top-10 chart and went platinum. The album also spawned his most famous song, "You'll Never Find Another Love Like Mine" which topped R&B charts and reached No. 1 on Pop charts.

Along with a successful singing an acting career, Rawls was also a major philanthropist within the African-American community. In 1980, he began the "Lou Rawls Parade of Stars" Telethon, an annual show he used to raise hundreds of millions of dollars for the United Negro College Fund (UNCF). Along with musical performances from various recording artists in support of his efforts, he raised over $250 million for college students across the Unites States to obtain a higher education.

Count Basie

Major Awards	Wins
Grammy Awards	9
American Music Awards	2
NAACP Image Award	1

Major Hall of Fame Inductions

Grammy Lifetime Achievement
Grammy Hall of Fame
Long Island Music Hall of Fame
Blues Hall of Fame
Hollywood Walk of Fame
Honored on U.S. Postal Stamp

One of Jazz music's all-time greats, Bandleader and Pianist, Count Basie (1904 - 1984) was instrumental in forming the "Big Band Sound" that characterized Jazz in the mid-20th century. Helping to define the era of "Swing" with hits like "One O'Clock Jump" and "Blue Skies," Basie became the first African-American male to win a Grammy Award. He was also the first African-American to have a band give a command performance before Queen Elisabeth. He lead his Jazz Orchestra for nearly 50 years. Along with his band becoming highly distinguished for its soloists, rhythm section and style of swing, Basie himself was noted for his understated yet captivating style of piano playing and precise, impeccable musical leadership. He also led one of the largest, most renowned African-American Jazz groups of his day.

Jazz Pianist, Organist, Bandleader and Composer, William James Basie, better known as Count Basie was one of the greatest Jazz musicians in history, he was noted for his piano style and leadership of influential and widely heralded orchestras. Growing up in Red Bank, New Jersey, both of his parents were musicians, his father Harvey played the mellophone and his mother Lillian was a pianist who gave her son his first lessons. After moving to Harlem, he was further influenced by renowned pianists, James P. Johnson and Fats Waller, with Waller later teaching Basie organ-playing techniques.

In 1925, he began his professional career touring with several acts to the cities of St. Louis, New Orleans, Chicago and Kansas City. In 1927, he settled in Kansas City, joining bandleader, Bennie Moten's band as a pianist. Basie was inspired by Moten's ambition to raise his band to the level of Duke Ellington's or Fletcher Henderson's.

Upon Moten's untimely death in 1935, Basie worked as a soloist before leading his own band called the "Barons of Rhythm." Many former members of the Moten band joined his nine-piece outfit, among them Walter Page (bass), Freddie Green (guitar), Jo Jones (drums), Lester Young (tenor saxophone) and singer, Jimmy Rushing. The band gained a residency at the "Reno Club" in Kansas City and began broadcasting on the radio, an announcer dubbed the bands pianist as "Count" Basie.

Basie received his big break when one of his broadcasts was heard by record producer, John Hammond, who touted him to agents and record companies. As a result, Basie's band made its recording debut on "Decca Records" in 1937. Their signature recording "One O'Clock Jump" became the theme song of the his orchestra, they used it to close each of their concerts for the next 50 years, later listed by the "Recording Industry Association of America" (RIAA) as one of the "Songs of the Century."

Basie then took his orchestra to New York City, Hammond introduced him to Jazz legend, Billie Holiday, whom Basie invited to sing with the band. The band made their first appearance with Holiday as his lead vocalist at the Apollo Theater. Basie always favored Blues musicians, he showcased some of the most notable Blues singers of the era while in New York, including, Holiday, Jimmy Rushing, Big Joe Turner, and Helen Humes.

Berry Gordy

Major Awards	Wins
Architect of Sound Award	1
American Music Award	1
Industry Icon Award	1
Grammys Trustee Award	1
BET Honors Award	1
National Medal of Arts	1

Major Hall of Fame Inductions

Grammy Hall of Fame
Songwriter's Hall of Fame
Hollywood Walk of Fame

Berry Gordy (1929 -) is the founder of "Motown Records," the hit-making enterprise that nurtured the careers of Diana Ross, Stevie Wonder, The Temptations, Michael Jackson, Smokey Robinson and countless other musical legends. The "Motown Sound" reached out across a racial divide, while politically and socially transforming popular music. As a songwriter, Gordy has written and co-written more than 240 songs for his music publishing company's catalogue. He is also a producer, director, entrepreneur, teacher and visionary who was actively involved in the civil rights movement, releasing an LP of the recorded speeches of Dr. Martin Luther King, Jr. entitled "The Great March to Freedom." Through his production company, "Motown Productions," Gordy also directed the films, "Mahogany" and "Lady Sings the Blues," which garnered a combined 6 Academy Award nominations.

Record Executive, Producer, Songwriter and the founder of Motown Records, Berry Gordy is responsible for starting the careers of countless musical icons of the 20th century. Growing up in Detroit, Michigan, Gordy dropped out of high school in order to pursue a boxing career before joining the U.S. Army. Shortly thereafter, he returned to Detroit to open a record store and begin producing recordings of his own compositions.

By the time Gordy founded Motown, he had already discovered Smokey Robinson who fronted the group "The Miracles," he then purchased a house at 2648 West Grand Boulevard in Detroit, naming it "Hitsville USA." During the 1960's Motown produced a string of hits that included "Martha and the Vandellas," "Dancing in the Street" and "The Temptations" "My Girl," Gordy also developed "The Supremes" as Motown's first superstar act. The group become the most successful female singing trio of all time.

There was an endless number of young, talented artists from the area who began to show up at Hitsville. Gordy set up an environment of stiff competition, where artists and producers were constantly trying to outdo one another. The strategy worked, and the company had hit after hit during the early 1960's with songs, like "My Guy," that broke the color barrier, reaching not just the African-American radio stations, but going to other stations and succeeding among Caucasian audiences as well.

In the early 1970's Gordy relocated the company to Hollywood, California and began producing motion pictures, including "Lady Sings the Blues" (1972), starring Ross in her film debut as singer, Billie Holiday. Gordy also produced and directed the film, "Mahogany," (1975). During the 1980's the company boasted annual revenues in excess of $100 million, and Motown acts had recorded more than 50 No. 1 hits on the Billboard Pop singles chart. Gordy wrote or co-wrote over 240 of the approximately 15,000 songs in Motown's music catalogue.

Gordy began the company with an $800 loan from his family, he turned Motown into the most successful African-American owned record label in history. In the process, he brought the world countless memorable songs, not only through his vision for spotting talent in others, but also his own talent as a songwriter and producer.

Etta James

Major Awards	Wins
Grammy Awards	6
Blues Music Awards	17
NAACP Image Award	1

Major Hall of Fame Inductions

Rock & Roll Hall of Fame
Grammy Lifetime Achievement
Grammy Hall of Fame
Blues Hall of Fame
Hollywood Walk of Fame

There are few female R&B stars that have enjoyed the kind of consistent acclaim that singer, Etta James (1938 - 2012) has received throughout her career, which has spanned for more than six decades. Often referred to as "The Greatest of all modern Blues singers," she has recorded a number of enduring hits, including "Tell Mama," "I'd Rather Go Blind," "All I Could Do Was Cry" and her signature recording "At Last." James possessed one of the most powerful voices in music, she gained the attention of the mainstream audience while scoring more than 30 R&B hits. She also had tremendous influence on "The Rolling Stones," Diana Ross and an entire generation of musical legends. Rolling Stone Magazine ranked James as No. 22 on its list of the "100 Greatest Vocalists of All Time."

Hailed as one of the greatest Blues singers in history, Jamesetta Hawkins, best known as Etta James has performed in various genres during her career, including Blues, R&B, Soul, Rock & Roll, Jazz, and Gospel. James received her first professional vocal training at the tender age of 5 from the musical director of the Echoes of Eden choir at the St. Paul Baptist Church, in her hometown of South-Central Los Angeles.

Growing up, her love of music grew stronger, she began listening to Doo-wop songs and was inspired to form her own singing group. James formed a female Doo-wop trio called "The Creolettes," who were later renamed to "The Peaches" after the girls attracted the attention of famed bandleader, Johnny Otis (who discovered James when she was 14 years old). In 1954, the group's song, "Roll with Me Henry" was an instant success. James celebrated her first hit single at the age of 15, she was also dating Blues legend, B.B. King at the time. A year later King's hit single "Sweet Sixteen" was dedicated to her.

After signing with "Chess Records" in 1960, James became their first major female star to have hit songs including, "All I Could Do Was Cry," "Trust in Me," "Something's Got a Hold on Me" and her signature song, "At Last." In 1967, she hit the charts again with the searing Soul song "Tell Mama." In 1976, James left Chess in order to pursue a solo career recording for other labels and perform on tour. She then became the opening act for Rock band, "The Rolling Stones" in the 1970's and 1980's.

James spent several years touring small clubs, she began working with new producers while embracing a style that combined her passion of R&B along with Jazz. After 7 years without a recording contract, James released the album, "Seven Year Itch" (1988) on "Island Records." She continued to record at an accelerated pace and found herself elevated to the status of R&B legend.

In 1994, she recorded "Mystery Lady: Songs of Billie Holiday," a tribute to the great vocalist she had long cited as a key influence in her life. Between 1995 and 2003, James recorded 8 albums, maintained a busy touring schedule and published her autobiography, "Rage to Survive: The Etta James Story." Having recorded more than 30 albums during her 60 year career, the popularity of her music continues to grow each day worldwide.

91

Miles Davis

Major Awards	Wins
Grammy Awards	8
American Book Award	1
NAACP Image Award	1

Major Hall of Fame Inductions

Rock & Roll Hall of Fame
Grammy Hall of Fame
St. Louis Walk of Fame
Hollywood Walk of Fame
Honored on U.S. Postal Stamp

Widely considered as one of the most influential musicians of the 20th century, Miles Davis (1926 - 1991) was at the forefront of several major developments in Jazz music, including Bebop, Cool Jazz and Jazz fusion. Many well known musicians rose to prominence as members of his ensembles. Throughout his life, he was at the helm of a changing concept of Jazz. In a career spanning over five decades, his music was truly groundbreaking and influential. The U.S. House of Representatives recognized and commemorated his album, "Kind of Blue" as a national treasure and encouraged the United States Government to preserve and advance the art form of Jazz music.

Jazz Trumpeter, Bandleader and Composer, Miles Davis is among the most influential and acclaimed figures in the history of Jazz music during the 20th century. Growing up in Alton, Illinois, Davis had a love for music at a young age. On his 13th birthday, his father bought him a new trumpet. Davis played professionally while in high school. When he was 17 years old, he was invited by Jazz legends, Dizzy Gillespie and Charlie Parker to join them onstage when the famed musicians realized they needed a trumpet player to replace a sick bandmate.

In 1944, his father encouraged him study at "The Institute of Musical Arts," which later became known as "The Juilliard School" in New York City. While taking courses at Juilliard, Davis reached out to Charlie Parker in order to see if he could join his band while they performed local gigs at Harlem nightclubs. During his performances, he built a relationship with several other musicians whom he would later perform with. They would would all eventually form the basis for "Bebop," (a fast, improvisational style of Jazz that was instrumental in defining the modern Jazz era).

Between 1945 and 1948, Davis and Parker recorded continuously, Davis built a reputation for his improvisational style that defined his trumpet playing. In 1949, he formed a nine-piece band with uncommon additions, such as the french horn, trombone and tuba. He released a series of singles that would later be considered a significant contribution to modern Jazz, they were later released as part of the album, "Birth of the Cool."

Davis and his band recorded several albums during the 1950's, including "Porgy and Bess" and "Kind of Blue." Now considered one of the greatest Jazz albums ever recorded, Kind of Blue is credited as the largest-selling Jazz album of all time, selling more than 2 million copies worldwide.

During the 1960's, Davis continued to be successful as his band transformed over time, largely due to new band members and changes in style. His various band members went on to become some of the most influential musicians of the Jazz fusion era. The development of Jazz fusion was influenced by artists such as "Jimi Hendrix" and "Sly and the Family Stone." The 1969 Woodstock Music Festival, set the stage for the Jazz fusion movement to follow. Davis also became the first Jazz artist featured on the cover of Rolling Stone Magazine.

Donna Summer

Major Awards   **Wins**

Major Awards	Wins
Grammy Awards	5
American Music Awards	6
NAACP Image Award	1
Academy Award	1

Major Hall of Fame Inductions

Rock & Roll Hall of Fame
Dance Music of Fame
Hollywood Walk of Fame

Known as "The Queen of Disco" and the "Mother of Modern Dance Music," multi-talented vocalist, Donna Summer (1948 - 2012) gained prominence and notoriety during the "Disco" era of the 1970's. Pushing boundaries, she symbolized a time that her hard work transcended. Her number of hits included "Love to Love You Baby," "I Feel Love," "Last Dance," "Bad Girls," "Hot Stuff" and her signature song, "She Works Hard for the Money." Summer was the first artist to have 3 consecutive double albums hit No. 1 on the Billboard charts, she was also the first female artist to have 4 No. 1 hit singles in a 13-month period. Over the course of her legendary career, Summer's music gained a global following, she has sold over 130 million records worldwide, making her one of the world's best-selling artists of all time.

Singer, Songwriter and Actress, commonly referred to as "The Queen of Disco," LaDonna Gaines, better known as Donna Summer was one of the most influential Disco and Dance artist of the 20th century. Raised by devout Christian parents in Boston, Massachusetts, Summer was influenced by Gospel Icon, Mahalia Jackson, she began singing in church at the tender age of 10. While performing her first solo in church, Summer said she received an epiphany from God to use her voice to become a star.

In 1967, at the age of 18, only weeks before her high school graduation, Summer auditioned for, and was selected in a production of "Hair," The American Tribal Love-Rock Musical scheduled to run in Munich, Germany. Overcoming her father's initial objections, she accepted the part and flew to Munich with her parents reluctant approval. Summer learned to speak fluent German within a few months. After Hair finished its run, she decided to remain in Munich, where she appeared in several other musicals and worked in a recording studio singing backup vocals and recording demos.

In 1974, while still in Munich, Summer recorded her first solo album, "Lady of the Night," which scored a major European hit with the single "The Hostage." She then co-wrote and recorded a demo version of a seductive Disco track called "Love to Love You Baby," the final version of the song was released in the United States and it was an unprecedented 17 minutes long. The record breaking Disco track became an overnight sensation, skyrocketing to No. 2 on the Billboard chart.

In 1976, Summer released 2 albums, "A Love Trilogy" and "Four Seasons of Love," both of which were enormous successes. In 1977, she released 2 more hit albums, "I Remember Yesterday" and "Once Upon a Time." Her single "Last Dance" from the soundtrack of the motion picture "Thank God It's Friday," won the Academy Award for "Best Original Song."

In 1978, Summer then released her first No. 1 single for the song titled, "MacArthur Park." A year later, she achieved massive commercial success with her album "Bad Girls," which instantly scored 2 No. 1 singles, "Bad Girls" and "Hot Stuff," making Summer the first female artist to score 3 No. 1 songs in a single calendar year. Earning the title of "Queen of Disco" in the 1980's, she scored her biggest hit of the decade with "She Works Hard for the Money."

Quincy Jones

Major Awards	Wins
Grammy Awards	28
Emmy Award	1
NAACP Image Awards	3
NAACP Spingarn Medal	1
Tony Award	1
Soul Train Music Award	1
BET Award	1

Major Hall of Fame Inductions

Rock & Roll Hall of Fame
Grammy Living Legend Award
Songwriter's Hall of Fame
Hollywood Walk of Fame

Music Conductor, Producer, Arranger, Film Composer, Television Producer, and Trumpeter, Quincy Jones (1933 -) is one of the most iconic music producers of the 20th century. He has dominated the entertainment industry for six decades earning a staggering 80 Grammy Award nominations. Jones was the first African-American to be nominated for an Academy Award for two categories, including, "Best Original Song" and "Best Original Score" for his work on the music for the 1967 motion picture "In Cold Blood." Jones was the producer of Michael Jackson's record breaking albums, "Off the Wall" (1979), "Thriller" (1982) and "Bad" (1987). He has also been named as one of the most influential Jazz musicians of the 20th century by Time magazine.

Musical Performer, Producer, Arranger and Composer whose work encompasses virtually all forms of Popular music, Quincy Jones is one of the most successful producers in the history of music, television and film entertainment. Growing up in Seattle, Washington, Jones began studying the trumpet while he sang in a Gospel quartet at the age of 12. His musical studies continued at the prestigious Berklee College of Music in Boston, Massachusetts, where he remained until the opportunity arose to tour with Lionel Hampton's band as a trumpeter, arranger and occasional pianist.

In 1951, he moved to New York City where he built a reputation as an arranger, he was arranging and recording for several diverse artists, many whom went on to become musical icons, including, Sarah Vaughan, Ray Charles, Count Basie, Duke Ellington and Dinah Washington. Jones won the first of his many Grammy Awards in 1963, for his Count Basie arrangement "I Can't Stop Loving You." He then became the new Vice-President of "Mercury Records," making him the first high-level African-American Executive of an established major record company. Toward the end of his association with the label, Jones turned his attention to another musical arena, which was the world of film scores.

In 1985, Jones produced Steven Spielberg's adaptation of Alice Walker's "The Color Purple," which garnered 11 Academy Award nominations, introduced actresses, Whoopi Goldberg and Oprah Winfrey to film audiences, this marked his debut as a film producer. In 1990, He formed "Quincy Jones Entertainment" (QJE), a co-venture with Time Warner, Inc. The new company in which he served as chairman and CEO, produced the NBC Television show "The Fresh Prince Of Bel Air" and Fox Television show "Mad TV." He is also the founder and publisher of "VIBE Magazine."

Celebrating more than 60 years of performing and being involved in music, his creative magic as a businessman, television and movie producer has continuing through the high-technology, international multi-media hybrids. As the first African-American composer to be embraced by the Hollywood establishment in the 1960's, he helped refresh music in motion pictures with infusions of Jazz and Soul. His landmark 1989 album, "Back on the Block," brought legends such as Dizzy Gillespie, Ella Fitzgerald and Miles Davis together with a new generation of Hip-Hop artist. Jones stands as the most successful and admired executive in the entertainment world.

Dizzy Gillespie

Major Awards	Wins
Grammy Awards	2
Golden Globe Award	1

Major Hall of Fame Inductions

Rock & Roll Hall of Fame
Grammy Lifetime Achievement
Grammy Hall of Fame
Jazz Hall of Fame
New Jersey Hall of Fame
National Medal of Arts
Hollywood Walk of Fame

Known for his famous swollen cheeks and signature (uniquely angled) trumpet's bell, Jazz Trumpeter, Dizzy Gillespie's (1917 - 1993) effect on Jazz music cannot be overstated, his trumpet playing has influenced every player who rose to prominence after him. His compositions have become an integral part of Jazz music, and his bands have included some of the most significant names in the business. Gillespie, along with composer, Charlie Parker were the major leaders in the development of the "Bebop Movement." Known as "The Ambassador of Jazz," Gillespie's best-known works include the songs "Oop Bob Sh' Bam," "Groovin' High," "Leap Frog," "Salt Peanuts" and "My Melancholy Baby." In addition to being a renowned Jazz trumpet player, he was also a bandleader, singer, composer and teacher.

Jazz Trumpeter, Bandleader, Composer and Singer, known as "The Ambassador of Jazz," John Birks Gillespie, better known as Dizzy Gillespie was a major figure in the development of Bebop and modern Jazz music. Growing up in Cheraw, South Carolina, he began playing the piano at the age of 4, his father was a local bandleader, so musical instruments were made available to his children. Gillespie taught himself how to play the trombone as well as the trumpet by the age of 12. While practicing one night, he heard his idol, trumpet player, Roy Eldridge on the radio, from that moment on, he dreamed of becoming a Jazz musician.

Gillespie's earliest professional work included joining the orchestras of Fran Fairfax in 1935 and Teddy Hill in 1937, during this period he acquired the nickname "Dizzy" by which he has become universally known for. He later created his own band and developed his own signature style, working with musical greats like Cab Calloway, Ella Fitzgerald, Earl Hines, Charlie Parker and Duke Ellington. Gillespie's best-known compositions include "Oop Bob Sh' Bam," "Groovin' High," "Salt Peanuts," "A Night in Tunisia" and "Johnny Come Lately."

While on tour, another band member accidentally bent his trumpet in such a way that the upward 45-degree angle of the bell allowed him to hear the notes at a much better angle, he discovered that its new shape improved the instrument's sound quality. He enjoyed the unexpected sound effects of the bent trumpet so much that he ordered future customized trumpets constructed similar to the bent design.

Gillespie's trumpet playing was at a peak, with rapid-fire attacks of notes and an amazing harmonic range. His showmanship lead him to become the leading figure to popularize a new music called "Bebop." After years of perfecting his craft as a world renowned trumpet player, his cheeks began to balloon out of their natural shape due to being overused.

In 1956, President Dwight D. Eisenhower invited Gillespie and his band to participate on a State Department tour of the Middle East, Africa, and Asia, which earned him the nickname "The Ambassador of Jazz." In 1989, he had more than 300 performances in 27 countries around the world. In the history of Jazz trumpeters, Gillespie sound comes second only to Louis Armstrong.

George Clinton Parliament-Funkadelic

Major Hall of Fame Inductions

Rock & Roll Hall of Fame
Grammy Lifetime Achievement

Known as the "King of Funk," George Clinton (1941 -) revolutionized Funk and R&B music in the 1970's, he was the mastermind behind the group Parliament-Funkadelic (P-Funk). Nicknamed "Dr. Funkenstein," Clinton is known for his outrageous costumes and marathon live shows as well as his innovative fusion of Rock, R&B and Psychedelic dance music. During his career he has released more than 30 albums, including "Funkadelic" (1970), "One Nation Under a Groove" (1978) and "The Awesome Power of a Fully Operational Mothership" (1997). In a career that has spanned over five decades, he has personally collaborated with most of the groups and artists that have been influence by his music. Clinton has grown into a beloved cultural icon, his music has been sampled by hundreds of artists over several genres of music.

Singer, Songwriter, Bandleader and Producer, often referred to as the "King of Funk," George Clinton developed an influential and eclectic form of Funk and R&B Music during the 1970's. Clinton is regarded, along with James Brown and Sly Stone, as one of the foremost innovators of Funk Music. Growing up in Plainfield, New Jersey, during his teen years, Clinton formed a Doo-wop group inspired by "Frankie Lymon and the Teenagers" called "The Parliaments," based out of the back room of a barbershop where he worked.

In 1960, Clinton and The Parliaments relocated to Detroit, Michigan in order to audition for "Motown Records" as a Doo-wop group. The record label decided to hire Clinton instead as a songwriter. The Parliaments then signed a contract with another Detroit label, "Revillot Records." The group reached their apex with Revillot in 1967 with the hit single "I Wanna Testify." During a contract dispute, Revillot temporarily prevented the Parliaments from continuing under that name.

Clinton then renamed the group Funkadelic, seizing the opportunity of pushing the instrumentalists to embrace Psychedelic Rock without losing a grip on Soul and Funk. The group eventually found success under the name Parliament-Funkadelic (P-Funk). By the end of the 1970's, Parliament-Funkadelic had 7 platinum albums with a combined 39 charting singles, peaking toward the end of the decade with No. 1 hits including "Flash Light," "One Nation Under a Groove," "Atomic Dog," and "Aqua Boogie."

Clinton was also a notable music producer, he produced albums for several Funk legends during his career. In 1974, he regained the rights back to the name Parliament and then released the album "Up for the Downstroke." The album prominently featured Clinton's newest band member, bass player Bootsy Collins. Prior to joining Parliament-Funkadelic, Collins rose to prominence with singer, James Brown in the early 1970's. His bass guitar and humorous vocals established him as one of the leading names in Funk music during that era.

During the mid to late 1980's, many Hip-Hop artists cited Clinton's music as an influence. Along with James Brown, Clinton's songs with Parliament-Funkadelic are some of the most sampled songs in the history of music.

Smokey Robinson

Major Awards   **Wins**

Major Awards	Wins
Grammy Award	1
Grammy Legend Award	1
R&B Pioneer Award	1
Soul Train Music Award	1

Major Hall of Fame Inductions

Rock & Roll Hall of Fame
Grammy Lifetime Achievement
BET Lifetime Achievement
Songwriter's Hall of Fame
Hollywood Walk of Fame

Smokey Robinson (1940 -) was the man who first pushed America's most iconic Soul music label "Motown Records" toward greatness. As the leader of the group "The Miracles," he was the very first artist signed to the label in 1959. Robinson delivered 37 Top-10 hits with the group and also as a solo performer, he was also an invaluable behind-the-scenes talent who wrote songs, produced records, scouted and groomed talent, and served as a Vice President at Motown from 1961 to 1988. Robinson is one of the most iconic figures in R&B, his work helped defined Pop-oriented Soul, his lush romantic ballads literally gave the genre "Quiet Storm" its name. He is often referred to as "America's Greatest Living Poet." Rolling Stone Magazine ranked Robinson as No. 20 on its list of "100 Greatest Vocalists of All Time."

Singer, Songwriter, Producer, and Record Executive, William Robinson, best known as Smokey Robinson has been hailed by many as one of the greatest songwriter's in history. Growing up in Detroit Michigan, he was given the nickname "Smokey Joe" from his uncle Claude, which quickly stuck. He first developed an interest in music by investigating his mother's record collection, which included classics by Sarah Vaughan, Billy Eckstine, Muddy Waters, and John Lee Hooker. In his early teens, he began singing and performing in informal Doo-wop groups with his friends.

In 1958, Robinson assembled a vocal group called "The Miracles," a co-ed musical lineup who began making a name for themselves on Detroit's R&B scene. The same year, Robinson met Berry Gordy, a Detroit-based songwriter who penned several hits for singer, Jackie Wilson and was looking to make a name for himself in the music business.

Gordy was impressed with The Miracles and Robinson's talents as a songwriter, he helped the band land a deal with "End Records," and The Miracles released their first single, "Got a Job." Robinson believed he and Gordy could do better themselves, he urged Gordy to follow through on his idea of forming his own record label. The Miracles became the first group signed to Gordy's new record company, "Motown," and in 1960, their song "Shop Around," (written by Robinson), was the first Motown single to become a nationwide hit record. As Robinson became recognized as the creative force behind the group, their name was changed to "Smokey Robinson & The Miracles" in 1966.

Robinson also shared his talents with many other Motown acts, he wrote the songs "My Guy" and "The One Who Really Loves You" for singer, Mary Wells, "My Girl," "Get Ready," and "The Way You Do the Things You Do" for "The Temptations," "Ain't That Peculiar" and "I'll Be Doggone" for singer, Marvin Gaye. Throughout his career, he has written over 1,000 songs for the label.

Robinson's career as a singer/songwriter has spanned over six decades, as the frontman with The Miracles and as a solo performer, his consistent commercial success and creative contributions to the label earned him the title "King of Motown," he was awarded the Library of Congress Gershwin Prize for his lifetime contributions to popular music.

Wilson Pickett

Major Awards	Wins
R&B Pioneer Award	1

Major Hall of Fame Inductions

Rock & Roll Hall of Fame
Grammy Hall of Fame
Alabama Music Hall of Fame

The Classic Soul era of the mid-1960's was largely defined by crooners and shouters. Wilson Pickett (1941 - 2006) was an impassioned screamer and throat-shredding force of nature that helped define Soul music. He did a great deal to establish the sound of Southern Soul with his early hits, he released some of the decade's hottest dance floor grooves including, "634-5789," "I'm gonna wait till the midnight hour / That's when my love comes tumbling down," "Land of 1000 Dances," "Mustang Sally," and "Funky Broadway." Pickett described himself as a Gospel singer who sung Blues material, he noted the raw emotional delivery and the total command of the stage were all were common to Gospel preachers and singers. Rolling Stone Magazine ranked Pickett as No. 68 on its list of the "100 Greatest Vocalists of All Time."

Singer and Songwriter, Wilson Pickett was a major figure in the development of Soul music in the 1960's. His forceful, passionate style of singing (under the influence of recording stars such as Little Richard) was developed at an early age in the Southern Baptist church and on the streets of Detroit, Michigan. Born in Alabama, Pickett migrated in the 1950's to industrial Detroit, Michigan, where his father worked in an auto plant.

Pickett was a product of the Baptist Church, Gospel music was at the core of his musical manner and onstage persona. He testified rather than sang, preached rather than crooned. His delivery was marked by his religious conviction, no matter how secular the songs he sang. Pickett's switch to secular music came quickly, as a member of the R&B vocal group "The Falcons," he sang lead on the ballad, "I Found a Love" (1962), which was one of the songs that interested "Atlantic Records" producer, Jerry Wexler in Pickett becoming a solo artist.

After meeting with Wexler, Pickett traveled to Memphis, Tennessee in order to co-write a song with Otis Redding's collaborator, Steve Cropper of the band, "Booker T. and the MG's." The result was a smash single, "In the Midnight Hour" (1965), which sold over one million copies. From that moment on, Pickett was a megastar.

Thousands of bands covered "In the Midnight Hour" on-stage at concerts in the 1960's. He had a flurry of other galvanizing Soul hits over the next few years, including "634-5789," (1966) "Mustang Sally," (1966) "Land of 1000 Dances," (1966) and "Funky Broadway" (1967), all of which, like "In the Midnight Hour," were frequently adapted by other bands and sampled as dance-ready numbers.

Before leaving Atlantic, Pickett entered a new decade and enjoyed another run of smash hits, including "Don't Knock My Love" (1971), "Call My Name, I'll Be There" (1971), and "Fire and Water" (1972). He then teamed up with established Philadelphia-based hitmakers "Gamble and Huff" for the album titled "Wilson Pickett in Philadelphia," featuring the hit single, "Engine No. 9" which sold over one million copies. Pickett recorded over 50 hit songs during his career, musical legend, known as the "Queen of Soul," Aretha Franklin referred to Pickett as "one of the greatest Soul singers in history.

Sarah Vaughan

Major Awards	Wins
Grammy Award	1
Emmy Award	1
NEA Jazz Masters Award	1

Major Hall of Fame Inductions

Grammy Lifetime Achievement
Grammy Hall of Fame
Jazz Hall of Fame
Hollywood Walk of Fame
Honored on U.S. Postal Stamp

Regarded as one of the greatest Jazz singers of the 20th century, Sarah Vaughan (1924 - 1990) was one of the most important vocalist to emerge from the "Bop" era. While Vaughan never gained the public recognition of fellow performers such as Ella Fitzgerald or Billie Holliday, she is generally considered to have one of the greatest voices of her era and is credited with being a major force behind the popularity of Bop music. Some of her biggest hits include classics such as "Misty," "My Funny Valentine," and "Tenderly." Her determination and ability to fit in (despite her natural shyness) with the mostly male-dominated world of Jazz music earned her the nickname "Sassy." Along with a career that has spanned nearly five decades, Vaughan's flawless voice earned her the title "The Divine One."

Jazz Singer and Pianist, who was known for having one of the most amazing voices of the 20th century, Sarah Vaughan was a pioneer in the use of Bebop phrasing in popular songs. Growing up in Newark, New Jersey, she studied piano from the age of 7, as a teenager she became an organist and choir soloist at the Mount Zion Baptist Church. In 1943, 19 year-old Vaughan was ready to began her music career.

Despite her natural shyness and lack of stage presence, she won an amateur contest at Harlem's renowned Apollo Theatre. That performance led to Vaughan's discovery by singer, Billy Eckstine. Six months later, she had joined Eckstine in "Earl Hines Big Band" along with Jazz legends, Dizzy Gillespie and Charlie Parker. When Eckstine formed his own band soon after, Vaughan followed along, others including Miles Davis and Art Blakey. In 1947, Vaughan decided to pursue a solo career.

Having already been given the nickname "Sassy" as a commentary on her onstage style, it was while going solo she was dubbed as "The Divine One," she then released the recordings "If You Could See Me Now" and "It"s Magic." Vaughan expanded her Jazz repertoire to include Pop music. As a result, she enlarged her audience and gained increased attention for her formidable talent.

The next decade saw Vaughan produce more Pop music, she released hit songs such as, "Whatever Lola Wants," "Misty" and "Broken-Hearted Melody," which sold more than one million copies worldwide. Vaughan frequently toured in the United States and Europe, her singing was also featured in motion pictures such as "Disc Jockey" (1951) and "Basin Street Revue" (1956).

In the late 1960's, Vaughan returned to performing and recording Jazz music, her recordings of the "Duke Ellington Song Book (1 and 2)" are considered some of the finest recordings during that time. While she continued to work without the massive level of commercial success enjoyed by colleagues such as Ella Fitzgerald and Billie Holiday, Vaughan consistently retained a special place in the hearts of fellow musicians and audiences alike. Along with a career that spanned nearly five decades, remarkably, unlike many other singers, Vaughan never lost any of her extraordinary talent during her entire career.

Bo Diddley

Major Awards   **Wins**

Major Awards	Wins
R&B Pioneer Award	1
BMI Icon Award	1

Major Hall of Fame Inductions

Rock & Roll Hall of Fame
Grammy Lifetime Achievement
Grammy Hall of Fame
R&B Hall of Fame
Blues Hall of Fame
Mississippi Music Hall of Fame
Florida Artists Hall of Fame

Rock & Roll Pioneer, Bo Diddley (1928 - 2008) is known for developing many new musical styles and innovations. He was one of the first performers of the 1950's to incorporate woman musicians, he hired "Lady Bo," who became the first female lead guitarist in history to be employed by a major act. Diddley also used special effect manipulations of his distinctive rectangular shaped guitar, which made him an extremely influential musician. He danced around the stage while playing his guitar over his head, with his teeth, and even between his legs. His unique style would influence countless generations of future Rock musicians. He is the only musician in history to have a beat named after him, "The Bo Diddley Beat" which is a syncopated musical rhythm, that has been widely used in Rock & Roll and Pop music for decades since its introduction.

Singer, Guitarist, Songwriter and Music Producer, Ellas McDaniel, better known as Bo Diddley played a key role in the transition from the Blues to Rock & Roll music in the 1950's. Growing up in Chicago, Illinois, he was an active member of Ebenezer Baptist Church, where he studied the violin. Diddley soon began to play the guitar, his unique approach to guitar stemmed largely from his attempts to imitate the sound of a bow on a violin. As a teenager, he began playing in clubs with groups that included Blues recording artists, Jody Williams and Billy Boy Arnold, it was during this time that bandleaders gave him the nickname, Bo Diddley.

Diddley wanted to achieve his own sound, he rebuilt guitar amplifiers and constructed a tremolo unit out of a clock spring and automobile parts in order to enhance the group's rhythm by adding maracas and drums. In 1955, he recorded his first hit singles titled, "Bo Diddley" followed by "I'm A Man" (which was recorded as a bold declaration of African-American pride at a time) on "Checkers Records."

Soon afterwards Diddley began to tour, performing in schools, colleges, and churches across the United States. Regardless of the venue he taught people the importance of respect, education and of the dangers of drugs and gang culture.

Diddley was one most unconventional yet influential figures in the history of Rock & Roll music. He had something nobody else could claim, he created his own beat called the "Bo Diddley." The distinctive rhythm of his "Bo Diddley" beat and his pioneering use of electronic distortion were groundbreaking. Commonly dressed in a huge black "Stetson" hat and loud shirts, Diddley also influenced the culture of British groups such as "The Rolling Stones." The odd-shaped guitars that he played reinforced his unique look.

Diddley, Fats Domino, Little Richard and Chuck Berry were among the few African-American artists to achieve crossover stardom in the 1950's Rock & Roll market, many bands adopted Diddley's songs and beat, his guitar sound became part of the basic vocabulary of Rock music. He influenced guitarists such as, Jimi Hendrix, and Led Zeppelin's Jimmy Page, while his later Funk recordings have been sampled by several Hip-Hop artists.

109

Curtis Mayfield

Major Awards   **Wins**

Major Awards	Wins
Grammy Legend Award	1
R&B Pioneer Award	1
American Music Award	1
Soul Train Music Award	1

Major Hall of Fame Inductions

Rock & Roll Hall of Fame
Grammy Lifetime Achievement
Grammy Hall of Fame
Vocal Group hall of Fame

As the lead vocalist of the Soul vocal group "The Impressions," Curtis Mayfield (1942 - 1999) recorded some of the finest music of the 1960's. As a solo artist in the 1970's, he helped pioneer Funk music and introduced hard-hitting urban commentary into Soul music. During the civil rights movement, African-American students often sang his strong-hitting lyrics. With powerful songs like "People Get Ready," "Keep on Pushing," and "We're A Winner," he motivated and inspired the people who were fighting for equal rights and justice. His soundtrack for the motion picture "Super Fly" was praised for its socially conscious themes dealing with crime, poverty, and drug abuse. Mayfield was well known for injecting elements of social awareness into Soul music. Rolling Stone Magazine ranked Mayfield as No. 40 on its list of the "100 Greatest Vocalists of All Time."

Singer, Songwriter, Guitarist and Producer, Curtis Mayfield is considered one of the principal architects of Chicago-based Soul music during the 1960's and 1970's. Growing up in Chicago, Illinois, Mayfield was a self-taught musician, learning to play the piano and guitar at the age of 7, he then began singing with the Northern Jubilee Gospel Singers at his church. One of his greatest inspirations was legendary Blues singer, Muddy Waters.

Mayfield entered the music business in 1957 as a vocalist and guitarist with the vocal group, "The Impressions," whose other members were Jerry Butler, Sam Gooden, and brothers Richard and Arthur Brooks. Butler along with the Brooks brothers left the group in 1962 and was replaced by Fred Cash.

After the group was reduced to a trio, Mayfield, along with Gooden and Cash, devised a new vocal style, a three-part alternating lead, which allowed Mayfield's delicate high tenor to be balanced by Gooden's bass and Cash's low tenor. Derived from Gospel music, this switch-off technique called for each vocalist to take a turn with the lead part while the others provided backing harmony, it was later adopted by groups such as Sly and the Family Stone and Earth, Wind and Fire.

The 1960's proved to be the most successful decade for the Impressions. The group recorded 14 Top-10 hits along with a series of songs that were inspired by the civil rights movement including "It's All Right," "Keep on Pushing," "People Get Ready" and "We're a Winner." Besides achieving success during this period, The Impressions became the leading artists identified with African-American music that featured "social commentary."

In 1968, Mayfield became one of the first African-American artists to own a recording studio and production company, which were both located in Chicago. He also formed "Curtom Records" in 1970, an independent label that allowed him to write and produce hit records for artists such as "Gladys Knight and the Pips," Aretha Franklin, and the Staples Singers.

In 1970, Mayfield left The Impressions to pursue a solo career in the newly developing Funk music genre. Although he would record the commercially successful albums "Curtis" and "Curtis/Live!" his soundtrack for the motion picture Superfly in 1971 gained him the most worldwide recognition.

Thomas Dorsey

Major Hall of Fame Inductions

Grammy Trustee Award
Songwriter's Hall of Fame
Georgia Music Hall of Fame
Blues Hall of Fame
Gospel Music Hall of Fame

Known as "The Father of Gospel," Thomas Dorsey (1899 - 1993) founded the first Gospel Choir in the world along with Theodore Frye at Chicago's Ebenezer Baptist Church. He established the first music publishing firm, "Dorsey Music," dedicated only to Gospel music in 1932. Dorsey wrote more than 2000 Blues and Gospel songs during his lifetime. His song, "Precious Lord, Take My Hand" has been declared one of the most profound expressions of Christian Faith ever published. He also founded and became the President of the National Convention of Gospel Choirs and Choruses. Dorsey's songs have been recorded by several generations of musical legends such as Mahalia Jackson, Aretha Franklin, Little Richard, Josh White, and B.B. King, among others. He felt "Gospel is good music sent down from the Lord to save the people, it's what everyone needs."

Gospel and Blues Singer, known as "The Father of Gospel Music," Thomas Dorsey became a merging point for many musical styles in the early 1920's. Growing up in rural Atlanta, Georgia, Dorsey was the son of a Baptist preacher and his mother was the church organist, at the age of 6, he began playing the family organ. Shortly after he began writing his own music, and by age 13, he was playing piano and performing with several famous Jazz artists. In 1916, Dorsey moved to Chicago to study at the Chicago School of Composition and Arranging.

in 1922, he attended a Baptist convention at the Pilgrim Baptist Church, and was very moved by the musical preacher he heard that night. After his experience, Dorsey began coining the term, "Gospel Music," he then wrote his very first Gospel song. Throughout his early years he felt torn between sacred and the secular music. Although his beginnings were in the Jazz and Blues tradition, he was also influenced by music he heard through his religious affiliations. His first attempts to combine the two styles, which he started calling "Gospel Songs," was met with resistance from churches.

In 1931, Dorsey formed the Nation's first Gospel choir at Chicago's Ebenezer Baptist Church, he then wrote one of the worlds most famous songs ever recorded, "Precious Lord, Take My Hand." After studying music formally in Chicago, he put together a band for Blues legend, Ma Rainey called "The Wild Cats Jazz." In 1932, he became an agent for "Paramount Records," shortly after, he discovered future Gospel legend Mahalia Jackson. The two soon began touring together in the 1930's and 1940's.

His song "Precious Lord, Take My Hand" was often performed by Jackson, and was a favorite song of the Rev. Dr. Martin Luther King Jr. Over the next two decades, Dorsey traveled extensively, teaching workshops and leading choruses, while composing over 800 Gospel songs. He felt "Gospel is good music sent down from the Lord to save the people, it's what everyone needs."

Having already written several major Gospel hit songs, he teamed up with guitarist, Hudson Whittaker, the pair co-wrote and recorded the song, "It's Tight Like That," which ultimately sold 7 million copies, and inspired a new style which became to be known as "Hokum Blues." Along with writing over 2000 songs, Dorsey has also contributed to over 300 Blues records.

Patti LaBelle

Major Awards	Wins
Grammy Awards	2
American Music Award	1
NAACP Image Awards	7
R&B Pioneer Award	1
World Music Award	1

Major Hall of Fame Inductions

Songwriter's Hall of Fame
BET Lifetime Achievement
Apollo Theater Hall of Fame
Philadelphia Walk of Fame
Hollywood Walk of Fame

Known as "The Godmother of Soul," Actress and Singer, Patti LaBelle (1944 -) is widely regarded as "The Queen of Rock and Soul" music. She began her career as the lead singer with two groups, "Patti LaBelle and the Blue Belles," which received success on the Pop charts in the 1960's, and "LaBelle," which received acclaim and a mainstream breakthrough in 1974 with their single "Lady Marmalade." Her success as a solo artist began with her first No. 1 single "On My Own" in 1986. She is renowned for her passionate stage performances, wide vocal range and distinctive high-octave powerful voice. During the course of her career that has spanned more that seven decades, she has sold over 50 million records worldwide. Rolling Stone Magazine ranked LaBelle as No. 95 on its list of the "100 Greatest Vocalists of All Time."

Singer, Songwriter, Actress and Entrepreneur often referred to as "The Godmother of Soul," Patricia Louise Holte, better known as Patti LaBelle has enjoyed one of the longest careers in contemporary music. Growing up in Philadelphia, Pennsylvania, LaBelle began singing in her church choir at an earlier age. When she was 16 years old, she won a high school talent competition, this success led to her first singing group.

In 1960, LaBelle teamed up with friend Cindy Birdsong to form a singing group called "The Ordettes." A year later, following the additions of vocalists, Nona Hendryx and Sarah Dash, the group was renamed "The Blue Belles." The following year, the group partnered with record producer, Bobby Martin and scored a Top 20 Pop and R&B hit in 1962 with the single, "I Sold My Heart to the Junkman," and subsequently hit the charts in 1964 with renditions of "Danny Boy" and "You'll Never Walk Alone."

The quartet, now known as Patti LaBelle & the Blue belles, signed in 1965 to "Atlantic Records," where they released the hit song "Somewhere Over the Rainbow," before soon going on tour. In 1970, the group was renamed "LaBelle," and they pushed their music in a funkier, rock-oriented direction, they performed on stage in wildly theatrical, futuristic costumes. A year later, they became the first African-American group to appear at New York's Metropolitan Opera House. The landmark performance introduced their signature song, "Lady Marmalade."

In 1977, LaBelle decided to leave the group in order to pursue a solo career, releasing her self-titled debut album that same year. In 1983, she released her breakthrough album, "I'm in Love Again," which included her first Top-10 R&B singles, with "Love, Need and Want You," "If Only You Knew," and one of her many signature songs "New Attitude."

Throughout her legendary singing career, and appearing on Broadway in several Tony Award winning musicals, LaBelle has sold over 50 million records while also having a very successful acting career, appearing in more that 50 motion picture and television roles. Along with her passion for cooking, preparing meals and becoming a celebrity chef, she has also emerged as a successful businesswoman, having her own cooking show, selling millions of cookbooks, cookware and her own signature dishes.

Sammy Davis Jr.

Major Awards

Major Awards	Wins
NAACP Spingarn Medal	1
Emmy Award	1
American Guild Award	1

Major Hall of Fame Inductions

Grammy Lifetime Achievement
Grammy Hall of Fame
Las Vegas Walk of Stars
Hollywood Walk of Fame

Sammy Davis Jr. (1925 - 1990) has been entertaining fans ever since his father (Sammy Davis Sr.) took him on tour with a dance troupe when he was 3 years old. Having a lucrative career as a Singer, Dancer, Comedian and Multi-instrumentalist, Davis has appeared on Broadway, television and several feature films. Perhaps best known as a performer, Davis was also an active supporter of the civil rights movement during the 1960's, appearing publicly with leaders such as Dr. Martin Luther King Jr. and raising thousands of dollars in benefit concerts to support other civil rights activists. Later in his career, Davis was part of "The Rat Pack," a popular group of entertainers including, Frank Sinatra and Dean Martin, whom all starred in several motion pictures together such as "Ocean's 11" and "Sergeants 3."

Singer, Dancer, Comedian, Actor and Activist, Sammy Davis Jr. has been commonly referred to as "The Greatest Entertainer ever to grace a stage in these United States." Growing up in Harlem, New York, his parents Elvera Sanchez and Sammy Davis Sr., were both entertainers. They separated when he was 3 years old, and his father took him on tour with a dance troupe led by Will Mastin. Davis joined the group at a young age and they became known as "The Will Mastin Trio."

During the groups travels in the 1930's, the young Davis not only became an accomplished dancer but also a skilled singer, multi-instrumentalist and comedian, he was soon the star of the show. In 1933, he made his first appearance in a motion picture, dancing in the film, "Rufus Jones for President." In 1943, at the height of World War II, Davis was drafted into the Army. In his service, he joined the "entertainment special services unit" and found a love for performing in front of crowds while on the main stage.

After the war, Davis resumed his showbiz career. He continued to perform with The Will Mastin Trio as the star of the act, singing in nightclubs and recording records. His career began to rise to new heights in 1947 when the trio opened for singer, Frank Sinatra (with whom Davis would remain a lifelong friend and collaborator) at the Capitol Theatre in New York. A tour with singer, Mickey Rooney followed, as did a performance that caught the ear of "Decca Records," who signed Davis to a recording contract in 1954.

In 1955, his first 2 albums "Starring Sammy Davis Jr." and "Sammy Davis Jr. Sings Just for Lovers," were released to both critical acclaim and commercial success. This led to headlining performances in Las Vegas and New York as well as further appearances in motion pictures and television shows, including "Anna Lucasta" 1958, (co-starring Eartha Kitt), "Porgy and Bess" 1959, (co-starring Dorothy Dandridge and Sidney Poitier) and "The Frank Sinatra Show" 1958. Around this time, Davis also made his Broadway debut, starring in the hit musical "Mr. Wonderful" alongside legendary dancer, Chita Rivera.

By 1960, Davis was an international superstar, he became a member of the "Rat Pack," a legendary group of entertainers comprised of himself, Frank Sinatra, Dean Martin, Peter Lawford and Joey Bishop, the hard-partying superstars of the Las Vegas and Los Angeles nightclub scenes.

Thelonious Monk

Major Awards | **Wins**

Guggenheim Fellowship | 1
Pulitzer Prize for Music | 1

Major Hall of Fame Inductions

Grammy Lifetime Achievement
Grammy Hall of Fame
Honored on U.S. Postal Stamp

Thelonious Monk (1917 - 1982) is recognized as one of the most innovative pianists of any musical genre, he achieved a unique original sound that even his most devoted followers have been unable to successfully imitate. His musical vision was both ahead of its time and deeply rooted in tradition, spanning the entire history of Jazz music. Monk along with Duke Ellington shares the distinction of being one of the most influential Jazz composers of the 20th century. He is known for his improvisational style and many contributions to the standard Jazz repertoire, some of his signature classic compositions include, "Round Midnight" and "Blue Monk." Monk is often regarded as a founder of Bebop, although his playing style evolved away from the form. He was also one of the most prolific composers in the history of Jazz music. In 2006, he was also posthumously awarded the Pulitzer Prize for music.

Jazz Pianist and Composer who is known as one of the founders of Bebop, Thelonious Monk is one of the most influential and innovative Jazz musicians of the 20th Century. Growing up in Rocky Mount, North Carolina, his family relocated to New York City in 1922. Shortly after, he began learning how to play the piano at the age of 6. As a teenager, he toured the United States as an organist with a traveling evangelist group. Monk was raised in the midst of Gospel traditions and street music, he later studied at "The Juilliard School" in New York City.

In the early 1940's, he began working as a sideman with New York City Jazz groups. Eventually he became the house player (regular performer) at "Minton's Playhouse," a legendary Manhattan nightclub. While there he formed a working relationship with other musicians who later become future legends such as Dizzy Gillespie, Miles Davis, Charlie Parker, Sonny Rollins and Milt Jackson. Along with these artists, Monk became one of the creators of the "Bebop Jazz" tradition (Minton's became the birthplace of the Bebop movement).

In 1944, Monk joined the "Coleman Hawkins Quartet," and made his first studio recording, Hawkins was among the first prominent Jazz musicians to promote Monk's style of music. Many of his compositions were generally written in the 12-bar blues or the 32-bar ballad form, which became Jazz standards. In 1947, he decided to pursue a solo career, signing with "Blue Note Records."

Monk's style was appreciated by other Jazz musicians such as Miles Davis and John Coltrane. He released the albums "Thelonious Himself" and "Thelonious Monk with John Coltrane," which proved to be masterpieces that launched his career as one of the most acclaimed Jazz improvisers of the era. Monk would record other compositions such as "Epistrophy," "Straight No Chaser," and "52nd Street Theme."

Monk is widely accepted as a genuine master of Bebop music. His compositions constitute the core of Jazz, and are performed by artists from many different genres. Since he was always willing to share his musical knowledge with others, an Institute was created in his honor, "The Thelonious Monk Institute of Jazz" which was designed to promote Jazz education, as well as train and encourage new generations of musicians.

Chaka Khan

Major Awards	Wins
Grammy Awards	10
World Music Award	1
Trumpet Legend Award	1

Major Hall of Fame Inductions

Rock & Roll Hall of Fame
Songwriter's Hall of Fame
BET Lifetime Achievement
Apollo Theater Hall of Fame
Hollywood Walk of Fame

Known as "The Queen of Funk," Singer and Songwriter, Chaka Khan (1953 -) began her career as the lead singer of the popular group, "Rufus." A multi-racial band that skillfully moved across Soul, Funk, Rock, and Jazz, they reached the mainstream with the hit song, "Tell Me Something Good" (1974). Khan launched her solo career with releasing the singles, "Sweet Thing, (1975), "I'm Every Woman" (1978) and "Ain't Nobody" (1983). Throughout her legendary career that has spanned over five decades, she had the rare ability to sing in seven music genres, including R&B, Pop, Rock, Gospel, Country, World music and Classical, her recorded music has produced over 2,000 catalog song placements. Known affectionately around the world as Chaka, she has become a musical icon. Her timeless, classic and unmatched signature music has influenced and impacted generations of hit-making contemporary artists. She also has a street named in her honor in Chicago, (Chaka Kahn Way).

Singer, Songwriter, Actress, Entrepreneur and Activist, often called "The Queen of Funk," Yvette Marie Stevens, better known as Chaka Khan is one of the most dynamic and accomplished artists to debut during the early 1970's. Growing up in Chicago, Illinois, Khan made her professional debut at the age of 15, singing in a Chicago club. She also attended several civil rights rallies with her father, as a strong supporter of the movement, Khan later joined the "Black Panther Party" and was given the name "Chaka."

In 1971, she joined a band named "Rufus," which had attracted a large Chicago-area following. Working as a file clerk by day, she began performing with Rufus by night, when the lead singer, Paulette McWilliams decided to leave the group in 1972, an 18 year-old Khan took her place. Rufus was offered a record deal with "ABC-Dunhill" and Khan followed them out to California. In 1973, the group released the hit record "Tell Me Something Good" which catapulted Khan and Rufus to instant stardom.

After recording a string of hits with the group, in 1978, Khan made a successful transition to a solo career when she signed with "Warner Brothers." Her solo debut album came later that year with "Chaka Khan," an overwhelming hit record which debuted its first single, "I'm Every Woman." Khan then teamed up with singer, Aretha Franklin who produced her other hit songs including, "Clouds," and "What 'Cha Gonna Do For Me?" During this time, Khan also pursued her love of Jazz music. She brilliantly re-worked the classic song, "Night in Tunisia" along with the song's originator, Dizzy Gillespie on trumpet.

The song that made Khan an instant megastar and propelled her career into superstardom was "I Feel For You" (1984). The song was a massive hit, it also made music history for being the first R&B song to feature rapping, which was performed by pioneering rapper "Grandmaster Melle Mel," along with musical legend, Stevie Wonder playing harmonica in the background. Khan also topped the charts with other hit songs including, "This Is My Night" (1984), and the instant classic, "Through The Fire" (1984).

Throughout her career that has spanned over 50 years, Kahn has cemented her stature as a R&B legend, many of her recordings have become staples in the R&B and Jazz formats of radio programming, she has also sold more than 70 million records worldwide.

The Isley Brothers

Major Awards	Wins
Grammy Award	1
American Music Award	1
NAACP Image Award	1
Soul Train Music Awards	4

Major Hall of Fame Inductions

Rock & Roll Hall of Fame
Grammy Lifetime Achievement
Grammy Hall of Fame
Songwriter's Hall of Fame
Vocal Group Hall of Fame
St. Louis Walk of Fame

Established in Cincinnati, Ohio in the early 1950's, Vocal R&B, Soul and Funk Group, "The Isley Brothers" began as a trio, consisting of brothers O'Kelly Isley Jr., Rudolph Isley and Ronald Isley. Along with chart-topping hits such as "Shout," "Twist and Shout," "This Old Heart of Mine (Is Weak for You)" and "It's Your Thing," the group has experienced longevity with a career spanning over an unprecedented 70 years. The Isley Brothers are the only group in the history of music who were able to stay relevant throughout multiple genres and have a chart-topping hit song for 7 consecutive decades. Their music has entertained as well as inspired several generation of musical legends.

122

Vocal Group, The Isley Brothers have enjoyed one of the longest, most influential and diverse careers in the history of popular music. Their family history as entertainers spanned not only two generations of Isley siblings but also massive cultural shifts, which heralded their music's transformation from gritty R&B to Motown Soul to Funk.

The first generation of Isley siblings were born and raised in Cincinnati, Ohio, brothers, Vernon Isley, O'Kelly Isley Jr., Rudolph Isley and Ronald Isley were encouraged to begin a singing career by their father, himself a professional vocalist, along with their mother, a church pianist who provided musical backing during their early performances. Initially a Gospel quartet, until their brother Vernon had a tragic bicycling accident in 1955, Ronald was then tapped as the remaining trio's lead vocalist.

In 1959, the group gained Pop recognition with their song "Shout," followed by their 1962 hit song "Twist and Shout" which remained on Billboard Pop chart for 11 weeks. The Isley's then decided to began their own record company, "T-Neck Records." During a 1964 tour, they recruited a young guitarist named, Jimi Hendrix to play in their band, Hendrix made his first recording with The Isley's, the single was "Testify." Hendrix later went on to become the greatest instrumentalist in the history of Rock music.

The Isley's made the decision to abandon T-Neck Records and signed with "Motown Records" in 1965. The group had a hit song a year later with "This Old Heart of Mine (Is Weak for You)." Their sound was rawer than standard-issue Motown, they developed an increasingly funky fusion of Rock and Soul, most notably on the single "It's Your Thing" (1969).

That year, the Isley's also welcomed a number of new members as younger brothers, Ernie and Marvin, brother-in-law Chris Jasper, and family friend, Everett Collins became the trio's new backing unit. They scored hits with "That Lady," (1973), "Fight the Power," (1975) and "For the Love of You" (1975). Spearheaded by Ernie's hard-edged guitar leads, the group began incorporating more Rock material into its repertoire as the 1970's dawned. The group's career longevity is unmatched, The Isley's are the only group in the history of music to remain relevant throughout multiple genres and have a chart-topping hit song for 7 consecutive decades.

Muddy Waters

Major Awards	Wins
Grammy Awards	6

Major Hall of Fame Inductions

Rock & Roll Hall of Fame
Grammy Lifetime Achievement
Grammy Hall of Fame
Blues Hall of Fame
Honored on U.S. Postal Stamp

Muddy Waters (1913 - 1983) is undeniably one of the greatest and most influential Blues musicians who ever lived. Often referred to as "The Father of Modern Chicago Blues," he took Delta Blues and added amplified electric guitars (often backed with electric bass and drums) to create a new sound by arranging everything into a band format. An unrivaled singer of Blues and a remarkable songwriter, his recordings and live performances proved to be immensely influential in a number of genres, including R&B, Rock & Roll, Hard Rock, Jazz, and Folk. As a songwriter and guitarist, Waters was the leader of one of the strongest bands in Blues music (which became a new genre for a number of musicians who would become legends in their own right). He moved Blues music from the Deep South to the Midwest, injecting his music with a fierce, electric energy and helping pioneer the Chicago Blues style that would come to dominate the music scene through the 1950's, 1960's, and 1970's.

Singer, Songwriter and Guitarist, commonly referred to as "The Father of Modern Chicago Blues," McKinley Morganfield, known professionally as Muddy Waters was one of the most influential Blues artist to emerge during the 20th century. Raised by his grandmother in Rolling Fork, Mississippi, his nickname came from his childhood habit of mud play on the plantations. Waters developed an early interest in music in his teens, he began playing the guitar at the age of 17, he honed his skills under the apprenticeship of famed Bluesmen and mentor, Son House, who taught him about the basics of Blues singing, open tunings, and slide guitar.

Waters made the acquaintance of several famous Blues guitarists on the southern circuit within a few years. He relocated to Chicago in 1943 and became a major part of the city's Blues scene with his loud, crude and brash electric sound. His brilliant verbal imagery, sensual lyrics and bottleneck slide guitar work produced hits such as "Mannish Boy," "I'm Ready," "Got My Mojo Working," and "Rollin Stone."

In 1951, Waters established a full band with Otis Spann on piano, Little Walter on harmonica, Jimmy Rogers on second guitar and Elgin Evans on drums. The bands recordings were increasingly popular in New Orleans, Chicago and the Delta region in the United States.

The group then brought their electric Blues sound to England in 1958, which made Waters an international superstar. After the English tour, his fan base expanded and began to catch the attention of the Rock & Roll community. His performance at the 1960 Newport Jazz Festival was a pivotal point in his career, as it caught the attention of a new fan base. Waters was able to adapt to the changing times, and his electric Blues sound fit in well with the 1970's "Love Generation."

Waters was credited with taking Delta Blues and escalating it by cranking up the volume with electric guitars and amplifiers, while turning it into a band orchestration. Among those who were influenced by his guitar work were musical icons such as Jimi Hendrix, John Lennon, Keith Richards, Jimmy Page, Johnny Winter, Buddy Guy, and countless others. His thick voice along with his firm, appealing personality defined showmanship techniques of Blues music.

Sister Rosetta Tharpe

<u>Major Hall of Fame Inductions</u>

Rock & Roll Hall of Fame
Grammy Lifetime Achievement
Grammy Hall of Fame
Blues Hall of Fame
Honored on U.S. Postal Stamp

"Sister" Rosetta Tharpe (1915 - 1973) is a true pioneer and game changer, she helped shape the modern Popular music genre from Gospel music. Known as "The Godmother of Rock & Roll" and "The Original Soul Sister," Tharpe is one of the founders of Rock & Roll music. She was one of the few African-American female guitarists to ever find commercial success and the first artist to blend Gospel music with a secular setting. Tharpe was also an an innovator, known for using her powerful vocals along with her electric guitar during her performances, she influenced several generations of musical icons such as, Chuck Berry, Little Richard, Aretha Franklin, Bo Diddley, B.B. King and Jimi Hendrix among many others. Tharpe is considered the greatest Gospel singer of her generation.

Singer, Songwriter and Guitarist often referred to as "The Godmother of Rock & Roll" and "The Original Soul Sister," Rosetta Nubin, better known as "Sister" Rosetta Tharpe is one of the founders of Rock & Roll music. Growing up in Arkansas, her mother was heavily involved in the Church of God in Christ as a preacher, Gospel singer and mandolin player. As a child, Tharpe was encouraged to sing in church. By the age of 6, she was performing in a traveling evangelical troupe, singing and playing the guitar to audiences all across the South.

Tharpe and her mother then moved to Chicago in the mid-1920's, the duo continued to perform in their local church along with other religious events across the country. She was soon hailed as a child prodigy, attracting huge followings amongst church and Gospel communities. Chicago exposed Tharpe to the sounds of Jazz and Blues music, it wasn't long before she began to incorporate these styles into her Gospel music. In 1938, following a brief marriage to a preacher named Thomas Thorpe, (from whose surname she would craft her stage name) she and her mother moved to New York City. There she recorded her music for the first time, becoming the first Gospel artist to be recorded by "Decca Records."

Tharpe recorded the songs "Rock Me," "That's All," "My Man and I" and "The Lonesome Road," which were huge hit records and made her a virtual overnight sensation, she was one of the first commercially successful Gospel artists. The influence of Jazz and Blues can be heard in her early recordings, especially in her guitar solos, and she was backed by a Jazz orchestra rather than a traditional Gospel band. The mixture of Gospel lyrics with such up-tempo, worldly-sounding music, shocked and alienated many of Tharpe's more orthodox followers, however her secular audiences loved the new sound.

Tharpe was changing the sound of popular music, in 1938, she appeared at Harlem's "Cotton Club." During this time, performing Gospel music with Jazz and Blues bands in a nightclub venue was unheard of, while also a woman playing a guitar in such a setting was considered scandalous. In 1944, she recorded "Strange Things Happening Every Day," the song cemented her reputation as an extraordinary guitarist and showcased her incredible vocal skills. It was the first Gospel recording to make the Top-10 of the R&B chart, and it was deemed as the first ever Rock & Roll record.

Frankie Lymon

Major Hall of Fame Inductions

Rock & Roll Hall of Fame
Grammy Hall of Fame
Vocal Group Hall of Fame
Hollywood Walk of Fame

As the lead vocalist for the 1950's group "The Teenagers," singer/ songwriter, Frankie Lymon (1942 - 1968) became the first African-American teen heartthrob. The group's success inspired the formation of a number of youthful vocal groups including "The Students" in the late 1950's and "The Jackson 5" in the 1960's. Released in 1956, Lymon wrote the popular song, "Why Do Fools Fall in Love" which quickly became the No. 1 R&B song in the United States and the No. 1 Pop song in Great Britain. Music critics credit the song's success as the likely result of Lymon's agile, ingenuous, and utterly charming performance. The single remains one of the key songs by which the Doo-wop style is defined and remembered. The record was followed by his other signature song "Goody Goody."

Singer and Songwriter, Franklin Joseph Lymon, better known as Frankie Lymon became the first African-American teenage "Pop Star" in the 1950's. Growing up in Harlem, New York, Lymon developed a love for singing at the age of 12. In 1954, he heard a local Doo-wop group known as "The Coupe De Villes" perform at his school talent show. Lymon became friends with the lead singer, Herman Santiago, and he eventually became a member of the group. In 1955, the group's name changed to "The Teenagers."

The group would sing Doo-wop songs under the streetlight on the corner of 165th and Amsterdam. One day while rehearsing in a group members apartment, they were discovered by the lead singer of the Doo-wop group "The Valentines," Richie Barrett. While being extremely impressed with their performance, Barrett scheduled the group for an audition with record producer, George Goldner at "Gee Records." Shortly after, the group was signed to Gee as "Frankie Lymon and the Teenagers."

A few months later their first record, which included the songs "Why Do Fools Fall in Love," and "Goody Goody," were released, and made it to the top of the national charts. Lymon's vocals and performing abilities (wise beyond his years) not only made him the hottest singer in America at the age of 13, but The Teenagers were a group several notches above the competition. Known for his baby-face and love of show business, Lymon was ready to lead America's new youth movement.

In 1957, The Teenagers released three more singles which reached the Billboard R&B Top-10 list, "I Want You to Be My Girl," "Who Can Explain" and "The ABC's of Love." As the band toured in 1957, Lymon made the decision to pursue a solo career.

Though only together for a brief 18-month period, Lymon and the Teenagers exerted an enormous influence, spawning several "kid" vocal groups and providing initial inspiration to "Motown Records" owner, Berry Gordy to model his entire Motown production approach around Lymon's original vocal style. Diana Ross, Smokey Robinson and his principal protégé, Michael Jackson (whose early recordings with the Jackson 5 are virtual re-creations of the early Lymon sound, merely updated) all show the influence of Lymon and the Teenagers groundbreaking work.

The O'Jays

Major Awards   **Wins**

Major Awards	Wins
American Music Award	1
NAACP Image Awards	2
Soul Train Music Award	1
R&B Pioneer Award	1

Major Hall of Fame Inductions

Rock & Roll Hall of Fame
Grammy Hall of Fame
Vocal Group Hall of Fame
R&B Hall of Fame
BET Lifetime Achievement

Vocal group, The O'Jays rose to the forefront of the "Philadelphia Soul Movement" of the 1970's. Formed in 1958 in Canton, Ohio, members included, Walter Williams Sr., Eddie Levert, Eric Nolan Grant, Bobby Massey, William Powell, and Sammy Strain, who named the group after their manager, Eddie O'Jay. Over the course of their legendary career that has spanned over six decades, the group has defined R&B and Soul music with hit songs such as, "Back Stabbers," "Love Train," "Time To Get Down," "Put Your Hands Together," and "For The Love Of Money." Along with 29 studio albums, The O'Jays are regarded by many as Soul music's greatest vocal group of the 20th century and Philadelphia Soul's most popular and long-lived groups.

Vocal Group, The O'Jays were one of the greatest Soul groups in history. The group's origins dates to the late 1950's, when childhood friends Eddie Levert and Walter Williams began performing Gospel music together in their hometown of Canton, Ohio. In 1959 the pair teamed with school mates William Powell, Bill Isles and Bobby Massey to form a R&B group called "The Triumphs." Renaming themselves "The Mascots," they released the single, "Miracles," in 1961. After Cleveland disc jockey, Eddie O'Jay championed the group, they renamed themselves again, becoming "The O'Jays" in 1963.

Isles departed the group in 1965, and that year the remaining quartet released its debut album, "Comin' Thru." They first entered the R&B Top-10 in 1967, with "I'll Be Sweeter Tomorrow (than I Was Today)." Massey then departed the group in 1971, and the next year the group released the classic album "Back Stabbers," with the album's title track initiating a long string of hit singles, including "For the Love of Money" (1973) and the Disco-influenced Pop hit song "I Love Music, Pt. 1" (1975).

Released in 1975, "Survival" was another hit record, spinning off the R&B No.1 hit "Give the People What They Want." Their songs, "Family Reunion" and "Stairway to Heaven," found the group making concessions to the emerging Disco sound. Powell departed the group in 1977, and he was replaced by Sammy Strain, formerly of "Little Anthony and the Imperials," later Nathaniel Best and Eric Grant filled the role of third member.

The group kept plugging away hit records for several decades and never completely disappeared from the R&B charts, they released the albums "Travelin' at the Speed of Thought" (1977) and "So Full of Love" (1978), which produced their massive Pop hit, "She Use to Be My Girl." In 1987, Eddie LeVert's sons Gerald and Sean followed in his footsteps and formed their own successful R&B group known as "LeVert."

Both as a member of the group LeVert and a solo artist, Gerald LeVert helped keep the family name alive. In 1995, Eddie appeared alongside his son Gerald on several occasions and recorded an album of duets named, "Father And Son." He also became the spokesperson for the many organizations that promoted social justice, reaffirming the O'Jays long-standing commitment to social change.

Charley Pride

Major Awards   **Wins**

Major Awards	Wins
Grammy Awards	3
American Music Awards	2
Country Music Awards	2

Major Hall of Fame Inductions

Grammy Lifetime Achievement
Country Music Hall of Fame
Hollywood Walk of Fame

Country Singer, Charley Pride (1934 -) became the first African-American singer inducted into the Country Music Hall of Fame. During his extraordinary career, he garnered a total of 29 No. 1 Country hit songs. Pride first emerged as a talented baseball player, he played briefly for a minor league baseball team before trying out for the California Angels in the early 1960's, his career was cut short due to injuring his throwing arm. He then decided to pursue a career in music and launched his singing career. Discovered In 1962, by Country music stars Red Sovine and Red Foley, Pride relocated to Nashville in the late 1960's. Throughout his career, he recorded countless enduring classics such as, "All I Have to Offer You Is Me," "Is Anybody Goin' to San Antone," and "Kiss an Angel Good Mornin.'"

Singer, Musician and former professional Baseball Player, Charley Pride broke new ground in the 1960's by becoming the most successful African-American to have a successful impact for the hardcore honky-tonk Country Music sound. Growing up in Mississippi, he received his first guitar at the age of 14, but initially pursued a career as a pitcher and outfielder in the major leagues. Pride would always sing country songs for teammates on bus trips. In 1960, he moved to Montana, where he played minor-league and semi-professional baseball and performed music in local nightclubs.

After a disc jockey in Montana, introduced Pride to Country stars Red Sovine and Red Foley, Pride pursued a publishing and recording contract in Nashville, inspired and encouraged by those two musicians. When Pride relocated to Nashville in the mid-1960's, there were no other African-American country singers in the genre during that time. After more than a year of making a name for himself, he established himself as a Country music singer and received a recording contract with "RCA Records" in 1965.

Pride began working with producer Jack Clement, who previously worked with Country music legend, Johnny Cash and musician, Jerry Lee Lewis at "Sun Records" in the 1950's. From the release of his first single "The Snakes Crawl at Night" (1966) Country music audiences were drawn to Pride's rich baritone voice, the extraordinary clarity and affecting simplicity of his singing, as well as the traditional content of the songs he recorded.

Throughout his career, Pride recorded more than 50 singles that reached the Top-10 on the Country music charts, many of his signature songs were acknowledged as Country music classics. Among these hits were "All I Have to Offer You (Is Me)" (1969), "Is Anybody Goin' to San Antone" (1970), "Kiss an Angel Good Mornin' " (1971), and "Someone Loves You Honey" (1978).

Pride received multiple awards from the "Country Music Association," including "Entertainer of the Year" and "Top Male Vocalist" in both 1971 and 1972. He has also performed the national anthem at both the World Series and Superbowl. As an international superstar, Pride has performed all over the world and continues to tour regularly in the United States, Canada, New Zealand, Australia, The United Kingdom and Ireland.

Shirley Caesar

Major Awards	Wins
Grammy Awards	11
NAACP Image Award	1
Soul Train Music Award	1
Dove Awards	15
Stellar Awards	13

Major Hall of Fame Inductions

Gospel Music Hall of Fame
Grammy Lifetime Achievement
National Endowment for the Arts
North Carolina Music Hall of Fame
Hollywood Walk of Fame

Known as the "First Lady of Gospel Music," internationally renowned Gospel singer, Shirley Caesar (1938 -) is a musical trailblazer who has influenced a wide range of artists across several genres. As a giant in the world of spiritual music, she has made an enduring mark on American music and the sounds of Gospel. Throughout her legendary career that has spanned over seven decades, Caesar has released over 40 albums. She also had a successful career performing in theater, television and several motion pictures. As the Senior Pastor of her North Carolina Church, Caesar would often provide weekly sermons to her congregation along with having an outreach ministry, which provides food, clothing, shelter, toys for children and financial assistance to those in need.

Singer, Songwriter, Humanitarian and Actress, often referred to as the "First Lady of Gospel music," Shirley Caesar is one of the most successful Gospel singers of the 20th century. Growing up in Durham, North Carolina, her father James was well known in the Carolinas as the lead singer in the Gospel quartet group, "The Just Came Four," Caesar began singing with the group at the age of 10. Two years later, she began touring with evangelist LeRoy Johnson, who had a television show in Portsmouth, Virginia.

While still in high school, Caesar continued touring throughout the Carolinas. In 1951, at the age of 13, she recorded her first record, she then released the single "I'd Rather Have Jesus" for "Federal Records," After high school, she attended North Carolina Central College. While enrolled in college, she felt she was anointed by God to continue down the path of preaching the Gospel. She auditioned for a female Gospel group from Chicago called "The Caravans." They were so impressed with her performance, she was hired immediately. She then left school for a career of singing and ministry.

In 1961, Caesar released a solo single, "Hallelujah, It's Done," which incorporated a sermon along with the music, she began touring as a singing evangelist during downtime from The Caravans. Caesar's work on her own helped her develop a dynamic performing style, she then decided to launch a solo career. She formed her own Gospel group, "The Shirley Caesar Singers," and by 1969 they landed a record deal with "HOB Records." Caesar would also continue to reunite and perform with The Caravans occasionally throughout the years.

In 1971, Caesar became first African-American female Gospel singer since Mahalia Jackson to win a Grammy Award. From the mid-1970's onward, she was a dominant figure on the Gospel charts. During her legendary career, she released over 40 albums, participated in 16 compilations, 3 Gospel musicals (Mama, I Want to Sing and its two sequels), while also appearing in several television shows and motion pictures. In 1981, she launched "The Shirley Caesar Outreach Ministries" to help serve the needs of the people of her hometown of Durham. In 1987, she was elected to the Durham City Council, while also serving a pastor at the Mount Calvary Word of Faith Church.

Bobby "Blue" Bland

Major Awards   **Wins**

R&B Pioneer Award   1

Major Hall of Fame Inductions

Rock & Roll Hall of Fame
Grammy Lifetime Achievement
Grammy Hall of Fame
Memphis Music Hall of Fame
Blues Hall of Fame

Singer, Bobby "Blue" Bland (1930 - 2013) was a pioneer of a distinct form of R&B called "Soul-Blues," he was well known for his rich baritone voice, sensual delivery and sophisticated style. Bland was one of the greatest storytellers of Blues and Soul music, he had a string of hits in the 1960's including "Cry Cry Cry," "Turn on Your Love Light," "I Pity the Fool" and "That's the Way Love Is." Bland brought the sound of Gospel music into the Blues, he helped transform music of the 1950's into the "Soul Style" of the 1960's. He placed 23 Top-10 hits on the Billboard R&B charts between 1957 and 1975 and had a strong following on the "Chitlin Circuit" all across the South. Bland was also a trendsetter, his music has been rediscovered by new generations of musicians, many legendary Soul-Blues singers have borrowed heavily from his style.

Singer, Songwriter, Robert Calvin Bland, known professionally as Bobby "Blue" Bland, was one of the most popular, electrifying and influential R&B entertainers in the late 20th century, he modernized the genre by blending elements of traditional Blues, Gospel and Pop music. Growing up in Barretville, Tennessee, Bland and his mother relocated to Memphis in 1947.

Bland then began his career singing with a local Gospel group named "The Miniatures." Eager to expand his interests, he began frequenting the city's famous Beale Street, where he became associated with a circle of aspiring musicians, including B.B. King, Johnny Ace, Rosco Gordon, and Junior Parker, who collectively were known as the Beale Streeters.

In 1952, Bland joined the U.S. Army, upon completing his service in 1954, he returned to Memphis to continue to pursue his music career. Back in the Beale Street music scene he began touring with "Little Junior Parker," a regionally known Blues singer. Bland was then offered a contract by "Duke Recordings," he also had cut three singles that were released on "Chess Records."

In 1957, Bland released his first commercially successful song, "Farther up the Road," which reached No. 1 on the R&B charts. He followed it up with the song "Little Boy Blue" which also became a No. 1 and established him as a major artist in both the Blues and R&B categories. A string of hits in the 1960's including "Cry Cry Cry," "Turn on Your Love Light," and "I Pity the Fool" made Bland, along with B.B. King, the most commercially successful Blues artists of that decade.

Bland was greatly influenced by the Reverend C. F. Franklin, who was Soul legend, Aretha Franklin's father, who cried out biblical passages in what Bland referred to as a "squall." Bland began combining the squall with a his rich baritone voice, which soon became a cornerstone of modern Soul singing. Bland began touring nonstop between 1958 and 1968, he played more than 300 nights a year for several years in a row. In 1979, after experimenting with the Disco sound, Bland moved to "MCA Records." He recorded the monumental song "Ain't No Heart in the City," which has been rediscovered and sampled be hundreds musicians worldwide.

Ma Rainey

Major Hall of Fame Inductions

Rock & Roll Hall of Fame
Grammy Hall of Fame
Blues Hall of Fame
Honored on U.S. Postal Stamp

Widely regarded as "The Mother of Blues," Businesswoman and
Entertainer, "Ma Rainey," (1886 - 1939) was the most popular Blues
singer and songwriter of the 1920's. As an entrepreneur, Rainey
established her own entertainment company in 1917, she was one
of the earliest and most respected Blues performers in the South.
Rainey is recognized for coining the term, "Blues" music, she is the
first professional Blues vocalist and one of the most influential singers
of her time. For over three decades, her performances contributed to
the growing popularity of Blues music. As a pioneer female recording
artist, she recorded 94 songs for "Paramount Records" before 1928.
Along with her powerful vocal abilities and energetic stage presence,
Rainey has inspired an entire generation of musical legends such as,
Louis Armstrong, Bessie Smith and Mahalia Jackson.

Singer, Songwriter, Entertainer and Entrepreneur, commonly referred to as "The Mother of Blues," Gertrude Pridgett, who is known professionally as Ma Rainey is recognized as the first great professional Blues vocalist. Growing up in Columbus, Georgia, Rainey began her career at the age of 12, performing as a singer and dancer in the local talent show, "A Bunch of Blackberries," at the Springer Opera House. In 1904, she married singer, William "Pa" Rainey. The couple began touring the Southern theater circuit as a song and dance team that was billed as, "Ma" and "Pa" Rainey.

Throughout Rainey's extensive travels and performing while on tour, her ability to capture the mood and essence of the rural South is something she decided to incorporate into her songs repertoire (this pattern of incorporating various styles of entertainment were typical of early musicians during the time). While coining the term "Blues Music," she was one of the earliest and most respected Blues performers on the scene, earning her the title "Mother of Blues."

After 20 years of dramatic performances on the stage, Rainey signed a contract with "Paramount Records" in 1923, shortly after, the first ever Blues recording was produced. She recorded 94 songs between 1923 and 1928, including "See See Rider," "Prove It on Me," "Blues Oh Blues," "Sleep Talking," "Oh Papa Blues," "Trust No Man," "Slave to the Blues," "New Boweavil Blues," and "Slow Driving Moan."

Rainey's songs were recorded with a wide variety of the best contemporary musicians, including a young Louis Armstrong, Bessie Smith and Thomas Dorsey. As a compelling entertainer with a powerful voice, and a style both earthy and sophisticated, she continued to travel and perform, drawing large crowds throughout the South and the Midwest, her popularity kept her on the road through the 1930's.

Rainey earned a reputation as a professional while performing onstage and as a businesswoman. After settling in Columbus, Georgia in 1935, she became the owner of two entertainment venues, "The Lyric Theater" and "The Airdome," she also had interest in "The Friendship Baptist Church." Along with contributions to Blues music, Rainey's music has been added to the National Recording Registry, by the National Recording Preservation Board of the Library of Congress.

DJ Kool Herc

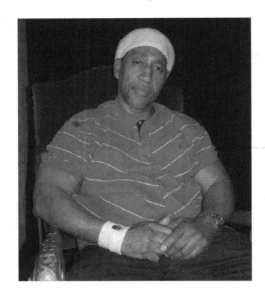

Often referred to as "The Founding Father of Hip-Hop," DJ Kool Herc (1955 -) was an innovative pioneer and creative force in the development of Hip-Hop and Rap music. Herc and his sister Cindy organized a "Back-to-School Jam" in the recreation room of their apartment block at 1520 Sedgwick Avenue in the Bronx, NY. There he originated a new technique called "Breakbeat Deejaying," (isolating and repeating the "breaks," or most danceable parts of records) by playing hardcore Funk records by James Brown and George Clinton using a two-turntable set up to emphasize the drum beat and switch from one record to another. Herc created the first prototype for modern day Hip-Hop music. Though others such as Grandmaster Flash and Afrika Bambaataa perfected and elevated the technique, Herc is credited for its creation. Since its introduction, Hip-Hop has evolved into a multi-billion dollar industry worldwide. Sedgwick Avenue was renamed "Hip-Hop Boulevard," as it was the birthplace of Hip-Hop.

Legendary DJ who is commonly referred to as "The Founding Father of Hip-Hop," Clive Campbell, who is known professionally as DJ Kool Herc is credited with helping to originate Hip-Hop music. Growing up in the Bronx, New York City, he was heavily influenced by the music of Soul and Funk legend, James Brown. Herc made a name for himself as a local DJ, he had a massive sound system which was capable of overtaking a party-goer's body, making them literally feel the music.

His younger sister, Cindy, became inspired to earn extra cash for back-to-school clothes, she decided to ask Herc (then 18 years old) to play music for a "Back-to-School Jam" for the neighborhood in their apartment building. Herc was notorious in his neighborhood for throwing all-night parties. The event took place on August 11, 1973 at 1520 Sedgwick Avenue in the Bronx and it became the birthplace of Hip-Hop music.

This was a monumental event, that night Herc developed the style that became the blueprint for Hip-Hop, he decided to use two turntables in a typical DJ setup in order to switch back and forth repeatedly between two copies of the same record, extending the beat to let the crowd dance longer to what they wanted to hear, he called this new technique, "The Merry Go-Round," (Known today as the Break-Beat).

His signature innovation came from observing how the crowd would react to different parts of whatever record he happened to be playing. During the event break-dancing also debuted, Herc coined the term for the dancers as "break-boys" or "b-boys." The event also contributed to the development of MC'ing (rapping and rhyming) over the microphone while using slang phrases. Inspired by a Funk recording, Herc encouraged participants to "battle" each other over the music while playing instrumental James Brown and George Clinton records. Brown's gritty, street-edged vocals, (a cross between singing and talking) also laid the foundation for Rap and Hip-Hop.

The event became known as a movement, the success of that party laid the foundation for a musical and cultural revolution. Six years later, "Rapper's Delight" was released by Hip-Hop trio, "The Sugarhill Gang." The single is considered to be the first song that popularized Hip-Hop music in the United States and around the world.

Charlie Parker

Major Awards	Wins
Grammy Award	1

Major Hall of Fame Inductions

Rock & Roll Hall of Fame
Grammy Lifetime Achievement
Grammy Hall of Fame
Honored on U.S. Postal Stamp

Charlie Parker (1920 - 1955) was one of the most important figures in the development of Jazz music, he is arguably the greatest saxophonist of all time. Parker along with Jazz trumpeter, Dizzy Gillespie were highly influential in the development the "Bebop Movement." As a pioneer of Bebop, he influenced generations of musicians, as well as sparked the fire of one of the most important and successful artistic movements in history. Parker's remarkable technique, original sound and ability to come up with harmonically advanced phrases were highly influential. By 1950, it was virtually impossible to play "Modern Jazz" music without closely studying Charlie Parker and his contributions.

142

Composer and Bandleader, who is known as the greatest saxophonist in history, Charlie Parker was a pioneer who lead a revolution in the development of modern Jazz music. Growing up in Kansas City, Missouri, during the 1920's was a time the city was a center for African-American music, including Jazz, Blues and Gospel. He discovered his own talent for music through taking lessons at public schools, by the time he was 12, he was playing in the high school marching band and in local dance halls.

Parker began playing with bands on the local club scene, he developed such a love for playing the saxophone, in 1935, he decided to drop out of school in to order to pursue a full-time musical career. From 1935 to 1939, he played the Kansas City nightclub scene with local Jazz and Blues bands. In 1938, he began touring Chicago along with his band. As Parker turned 20 years old, he longed to leave his hometown for New York City, where he was destined to go and change the face of Jazz music forever.

After arriving in New York, Parker joined "Jay McShann's Band," he began to develop his own original solo style and made a name for himself around town. In 1944, he then met young trumpeter, Dizzy Gillespie, they both later became members of the "Earl Hines Band." Gillespie and Parker became close friends and collaborators, they released the songs, "All the Things You Are," "Groovin' High," "Dizzy Atmosphere," "Shaw 'Nuff," and "Hot House." Although their music was a new sound, it resulted in Bebop arriving in full form on records, seemingly out of nowhere.

In 1945, Parker became the leader of his own band while also performing with Gillespie on the side, the two musicians launched a six-week nightclub tour of Hollywood, California. Together they managed to invent an entirely new style of Jazz, commonly known today as "Bop, or Bebop." Parker was engaged in some of the most rewarding playing of his career, leading a quintet that included Miles Davis, Duke Jordan, Tommy Potter, and Max Roach.

Parker's experiments in Jazz were also being heard worldwide, during his European tour, he was surprise to find his audience and following was just as large overseas. While visiting Paris in 1949, he was greeted by a thousands of fans. His European trips also encouraged him to expand his musical arrangements, including backing strings for both touring and recording.

Gladys Knight

Major Awards	Wins
Grammy Awards	7
Soul Train Music Awards	2
NAACP Image Awards	2

Major Hall of Fame Inductions

Rock & Roll Hall of Fame
Vocal Group Hall of Fame
BET Lifetime Achievement
Georgia Music Hall of Fame
R&B Hall of Fame
Hollywood Walk of Fame

Often referred to as "The Empress of Soul," Singer, Songwriter, Entrepreneur and Humanitarian, Gladys Knight (1944 -) was one of the most adored Soul singers of the 1960's and 1970's, she first rose to prominence as the lead singer of the group "The Pips." The group included her brother Merald "Bubba" Knight, and their cousins Edward Patten and William Guest. "Gladys Knight & The Pips" scored a series of highly successful hit singles for both "Motown Records" and "Buddah Records" from 1967 to 1975. Many of their signature songs included "I Heard It Through the Grapevine" (1967), "Midnight Train to Georgia" (1973), and "Baby Don't Change Your Mind" (1977). Along with a legendary career that has spanned over seven decades, Knight's gritty Gospel voice is considered by many to be one of the greatest voices ever recorded. Rolling Stone Magazine ranked Knight as No. 51 on its list of the "100 Greatest Vocalists of All Time."

Singer, Songwriter, Actress, Entrepreneur and Author, commonly referred to as "The Empress of Soul," Gladys Knight is considered as one of the greatest Soul singers in history. Growing up in Atlanta, Georgia, she first achieved fame in 1952 by winning "Ted Mack's Original Amateur Hour" television show contest at the age of 7. The following year, Knight along with her brother Merald "Bubba" Knight, and their cousins Edward Patten and William Guest formed a musical group called "The Pips," they soon began touring the country regularly.

In 1966, "Gladys Knight & the Pips" signed to "Motown Records," where they became part of Motown's Pop-Soul roster. Between 1967 and 1968, they had major R&B and Pop hits including, "Everybody Needs Love," "The End of the Road," "It Should Have Been Me," and "I Wish It Would Rain." The group was then developed into one of Motown's most dependable acts, responsible for 11 Top-10 R&B hits, including "I Heard It Through the Grapevine," "The Nitty Gritty," "If I Were Your Woman," and their signature song "Neither One of Us (Wants to Be the First to Say Goodbye)."

In 1973, the group elected to leave Motown for "Buddah Records," unhappy with the former label's shift of operations from Detroit to Los Angeles. While at Buddah, the group found immediate success scoring a series of highly successful hit singles including "Where Peaceful Waters Flow" and "Midnight Train to Georgia," In 1976, Knight made her acting debut with the leading role in the motion picture "Pipe Dreams for which the group recorded the soundtrack album. Knight was also responsible for sending the Jackson 5's first demo tape to Motown Records after seeing them perform at "Amateur Night" at the Apollo Theater in August of 1967.

Knight and The Pips continued to produce major hit songs until the late 1980's. They became one of the most prolific groups in the history of R&B and Pop music, they topped the national charts consistently with a total 55 entries in all. As a philanthropist and humanitarian, Knight's work included contributing to the NAACP Legal Defense Fund and her collaboration with singers Dionne Warwick and Stevie Wonder in 1986 for the iconic AIDS benefit anthem, "That's What Friends Are For." In 1989, she decided to branch out and pursue a solo career. Throughout the 1990's she continued to tour and release hit records as a R&B and Gospel music performer, which included another signature release, "Love Overboard."

Tyrone Davis

<u>Major Hall of Fame Inductions</u>

Chicago Blues Hall of Fame
Blues Hall of Fame
R&B Hall of Fame
R&B Pioneer Award

As one of the fathers of what music history has labeled as "Chicago Soul," Tyrone Davis (1938 - 2005) was known as the original "King of Romantic Chicago Soul, his stylish class made him especially popular with female Soul fans during his career that has spanned over four decades. Davis was a versatile baritone singer who could handle everything from Pop, Funk and R&B, but Smooth Soul was his most popular genre. He was known for his phenomenal body of recordings which includes more than 50 hit songs such as, "Turn Back the Hands of Time," "Turning Point," "Can I Change My Mind," and "Give It Up (Turn It Loose)." Davis is also regarded by many as a significant figure in Blues music, his legacy has paved the way for countless Soul singers for generations. Throughout his legendary career, he has sold over 25 million records worldwide.

Singer and Songwriter commonly referred to as the "King of Romantic Chicago Soul, Tyrone Davis was one of the most prolific Soul singers of the 1960's. Growing up in the small town of Greenville, Mississippi, he moved to Chicago when he was 19 years old. Chicago in the 1950's and 1960's was a hotbed of music. Similar to Davis, there were hundreds of African-American musicians that relocated north seeking a better life. They mostly all brought with them guitars and harmonicas, the musical traditions of Delta Blues and New Orleans Jazz.

Davis landed in the middle of the music scene, he spent his nights hanging out in Chicago's music clubs. In 1959, he eventually landed a job as a singer with legendary Blues guitarist Freddie King. In 1961, he went on his first tour as part of King's entourage. The more immersed he became in the music scene, the more Davis wanted to contribute to it. He noticed that most new musicians were attempting to sound like somebody already famous.

Davis instead embraced his own style of singing and began developing his distinctive voice, which was a quavering baritone punctuated by low-voiced growls along with a thick sensuality, allowing him to be noticed in a town known for good music. In 1967, Davis signed with "Dakar Records," a new label formed by Chicago music producer, Carl Davis. He released the songs "Can I Change My Mind" and "Give It Up (Turn It Loose)."

His next release, "Turning Point" allowed Davis to showcase his deep voice through its lyrics about relationships, it was a winning combination and the song flew to No. 1 on Billboard R&B charts and crossed over to hit No. 1 on the Pop charts. With over one million copies sold, the song became an instant Soul classic, it also cemented his reputation as the "King of Chicago Soul." He followed up with the song, "Turn Back the Hands of Time," which is widely considered one of the best Soul records ever recorded.

Throughout his career he catapulted onto the national Soul and R&B circuit of theaters, arenas and showcase nightclubs. His records consistently made the charts, outselling all of his Chicago Blues and Soul peers. Davis has sold over 25 million records worldwide and he has been among the many artists who proved that the Delta was a breeding ground not just for traditional Blues artists but also for Soul Singers.

147

Jimmy Jam and Terry Lewis

Major Awards	Wins
Grammy Awards	4
Soul Train Music Award	1

Major Hall of Fame Inductions

Songwriter's Hall of Fame
Hollywood Walk of Fame

In the 1980's Jimmy Jam (1959 -) and Terry Lewis (1956 -), emerged as the one of the most successful songwriter/producer teams in history. Their names are synonymous with success and their amazing catalog of hit records includes many chart-topping artist such as Michael Jackson, Aretha Franklin, Gladys Knight, Johnny Gill, Patti LaBelle, Mary J. Blige, Chaka Khan and New Edition. Defining the "Minneapolis Sound" that heavily influenced Pop music in the 1980's, Jam and Lewis were members of "The Time," a Prince affiliated Band that topped the charts with hits such as "The Bird," "Jungle Love" and "Cool." They later collaborated extensively with Janet Jackson, whose albums "Control," "Rhythm Nation 1814," "Janet," and "The Velvet Rope," changed the scope of Pop and R&B music forever.

Singers, Songwriters and Producers, James Samuel Harris and Terry Steven Lewis, known professionally as Jimmy Jam and Terry Lewis are the most successful production duo in contemporary music history. As longtime friends who met in an Upward Bound program for urban youth on the University of Minnesota campus, they created a body of work that has assured them a premier place in the Pop culture of the 1980's, and beyond.

In the mid-1970's, Lewis formed a band with Jam and Alexander O'Neal called "Flyte Tyme," they shared the funk spotlight with another homegrown Minneapolis superstar, Prince. Their band blossomed in 1981 when Jam and Lewis began regularly writing songs together. Around this time, Prince began exercising his entrepreneurial reach by essentially buying Flyte Tyme and replacing their vocalist, O'Neal with his friend and protégé Morris Day. Firmly in control, Prince dubbed the band "The Time" and began shaping them into a professional outfit. Although Jam and Lewis were the primary songwriters for the band, they were dissatisfied with their lack of independence under Prince's stewardship and decided to leave the group, while also realizing the benefits of the arrangement.

Over the next few years, Jam and Lewis developed their talents and built their business as both songwriters and producers. In 1984, they opened their own studio, naming it, "Flyte Tyme Productions," and set up a full-time operation in Minneapolis. Their production company reached the turning point in 1986, largely due to the success of Janet Jackson's debut album, "Control." Their work with Jackson exemplified the team's production ethic, demonstrating how they manage to realize the potential of musicians whose careers are at a crossroad.

Jackson lived in the shadow of her superstar brother, Michael, and received little attention despite years of work in television and music. Jam and Lewis approached her with a concept of designing songs specifically for her image and crafting an album to fill an apparent void in the music scene of the moment. Since then, the musical diversity and depth of their work as producers has been equally astonishing. They have generated millions in sales on over 100 albums, which includes an incredible 40 No. 1 Pop and R&B hits with artist such as Chaka Kahn and Patti LaBelle, among others.

Grandmaster Flash & The Furious Five

Major Awards	Wins
VH1 Hip-Hop Honors Award	1

Major Hall of Fame Inductions

Rock & Roll Hall of Fame
Grammy Hall of Fame

"Grandmaster Flash & the Furious Five" were a group of one DJ and five MC's that was instrumental in the development of Hip-Hop music. They were innovators who drove the birth of Hip-Hop on the streets and later in the clubs of New York City's South Bronx in the 1970's. During the early 1980's, as Hip-Hop transformed from being strictly live performances to recording records, the group released several groundbreaking songs such as "The Message," "Freedom," "The Birthday Party," and "The Adventures of Grandmaster Flash on the Wheels of Steel." They are widely regarded as the most influential Hip-Hop group in history. In 2007, the group became the first Hip-Hop artist to be inducted into the Rock & Roll of Fame.

Regarded as one of the most successful groups in the history of Hip-Hop music, "Grandmaster Flash & the Furious Five" consisted of members Grandmaster Flash (Joseph Saddler), Cowboy (Keith Wiggins), Melle Mel (Melvin Glover), Kid Creole (Nathaniel Glover), Mr. Ness (Eddie Morris), and Raheim (Guy Williams).

Flash, along with DJ Kool Herc and Afrika Bambaataa, pioneered the art of "Breakbeat Deejaying," (the process of remixing and thereby creating a new piece of music by playing vinyl records and turntables as if they were musical instruments). In the late 1970's, Flash began to develop a following and a reputation as a DJ, he was known throughout the five boroughs of New York for his house parties and block parties. He is also credited as the inventor of "scratching" (a technique of moving a vinyl record back and forth on a turntable to produce a rhythmic sound). This technique was soon mimicked by every upcoming DJ and became standard practice.

In 1978, there was a major shift in the realm of Hip-Hop, while still important, deejays began to take second place to MC's, Flash began recording rap songs, but he knew if he wanted to remain innovative and retain his flawless turntable technique he needed some help. He recruited a few of his friends Keith (Cowboy) Wiggins, and two brothers, Melvin (Melle Mel) and the older sibling, Nathaniel (Kidd Creole) Glover. They soon began writing their own rhymes and calling themselves "The Three MC's." Over time they added in Guy (Rahiem) Williams and Eddie (Mr. Ness) Morris and became the legendary group "Grandmaster Flash and the Furious Five."

In 1981, the group released what is considered the most influential display of cutting and scratching ever recorded, "The Adventures of Grandmaster Flash on the Wheels of Steel." Their song "The Message" changed the playing field for what a rap record could do, showing MC's they could create music other than party songs and still successfully sell records. The song paved the way for artist who would began to extract beats and melodies from existing records and combine them with a poetic lyrical delivery that would eventually become known as "rapping." The vinyl records and turntable used by Grandmaster Flash are on display at The Smithsonian National Museum of American History in Washington, D.C.

Kool & The Gang

Major Awards   **Wins**

Grammy Award   1
American Music Awards   5

Major Hall of Fame Inductions

New Jersey Hall of Fame
Songwriter's Hall of Fame
Hollywood Walk of Fame

Formed as a Jazz ensemble in 1964, vocal group "Kool & The Gang" became one of the most influential Funk groups during the 1970's, and one of the most popular R&B groups of the 1980's. Established in Jersey City, New Jersey, the group included Robert "Kool" Bell and his brother Ronald along with several of their neighborhood friends, Clifford Adams, Charles Smith, Woody Sparrow, Robert Michens, Dennis Thomas, Ricky West, and George Brown. During their legendary career that has spanned more than six decades, they have sold over 70 million records worldwide. The band's stellar reputation grew with each album, releasing party anthems such as "Celebration," "Cherish," "Jungle Boogie," "Summer Madness," Funky Stuff," "Hollywood Swinging" and "Joanna."

Vocal Group, "Kool & The Gang" are regarded as one of the greatest R&B and Funk groups in history. Growing up in Jersey City, New Jersey, their career began as high school friends who were inspired to create a Jazz band. In 1964, Robert Bell, his brother Ronald, and several of their neighborhood friends, Clifford Adams, Charles Smith, Woody Sparrow, Robert Michens, Dennis Thomas, Ricky West, and George Brown, formed the instrumental band called "The Jazziacs."

Robert who adopted the nickname "Kool" (due to his mild temperament) was 14 years old when he and The Jazziacs began performing in local New Jersey lounges. His father was a boxer who ran a gym on the upper west side of New York City, the gym was located in the same building as a music studio where Jazz legends, Miles Davis and Thelonius Monk (who became Robert Bell's Godfather) often performed. Their band went under several names before settling on "Kool and the Gang."

The group's attention to popular music transcended through 1960's Funk, 1970's Disco, and 1980's Pop and Synthesized sound. They had their first commercial success with the studio album, "Wild and Peaceful," which featured their chart-topping singles "Jungle Boogie" and "Hollywood Swinging," sold more than one million copies worldwide.

In 1979, the group added lead vocalist James "J.T." Taylor in order to move towards mainstream Pop and dance-oriented music, then releasing the album "Ladies Night, which had 2 Top-10 Billboard hot 100 songs, "Too Hot" and "Ladies Night." In 1980, their signature song, "Celebration" captured the Nation's mood of victory and soon became increasing popular worldwide. The song was often played over sound systems in packed stadiums and arenas, whether for sporting team victories or their own sold-out concerts. The single became one of the most copied and sampled songs of the late 20th century.

From 1988 until 1994 Kool & the Gang released 5 more albums, and began a world tour of Europe, United States, and Africa. Throughout their career, the group's global fame, recognition and following has spanned over six decades, due in part to their widely sampled catalogue. They are one of the most sampled bands in the history of music.

153

Whitney Houston

Major Awards	Wins
Grammy Awards	6
American Music Awards	22
Billboard Music Awards	11
Emmy Award	1
MTV Video Music Awards	9
Guinness World Records	15
Soul Train Music Awards	7
NAACP Image Awards	19

Major Hall of Fame Inductions

Rock & Roll Hall of Fame
Songwriter's Hall of Fame
New Jersey Music Hall of Fame
BET Lifetime Achievement
Hollywood Walk of Fame
Postage Stamp Honor - Grenada

Singer, Songwriter and Actress, Whitney Houston (1963 - 2012) is inarguably one of the greatest female Pop stars of all time. Her accomplishments as a hitmaker were extraordinary, she became the first artist ever to have 7 consecutive No. 1 hit singles, her 1993 single "I Will Always Love You" became the biggest song in Pop music history. Houston was also cited as the most awarded female artist in history by Guinness World Records, throughout her career that has spanned three decades, she became one of the best-selling recording artists of all time, with estimated sales of over 200 million records worldwide.

Singer, Songwriter and Actress, Whitney Houston has been entertaining fans with her soulful and powerful vocals for over three decades. Growing up in Newark, New Jersey, her mother, Cissy was one of the major figures in the world of Gospel music, and her father John was an aspiring singer who managed Cissy's career. Houston's extended family members include legendary singer Dionne Warwick who was her first cousin, and "Queen of Soul," Aretha Franklin was her Godmother.

Houston began singing at the age of 5 at New Hope Baptist Church in Newark where her mother was music director, she performed her first solo in the church when she was 11. That performance persuaded both Houston and her mother that she should become a professional singer. Her parents encouraged her to stay in school and launch a professional singing career after her high school graduation in 1981.

In 1985, 21 year-old Houston released her first album, "Whitney Houston," which sold more than 20 million copies worldwide and became the largest debut album in history at that time. Her single from the album, "I Wanna Dance With Somebody (who loves me)," entered the charts at No. 1, (which was the first single by a woman performer to ever do so). Her follow-up album, "Whitney," (1987), broke the record for having a total of 7 consecutive No. 1 hit singles.

Along with having a successful singing career, Houston decided to pursue a career in acting, starring as the lead role in the three motion pictures, "The Bodyguard" (1992), "Waiting to Exhale," (1994), and "The Preachers Wife" (1996). Her contribution to each movie soundtrack was monumental, recording the hit songs "I Will Always Love You" (which became the biggest single in Pop music history), "I Have Nothing," and "Shoop, Shoop."

After spending much of the mid-1990's working on motion pictures and their soundtrack albums, Houston released her highly anticipated first studio album in 8 years, "My Love Is Your Love" (1998). That same year she began a world tour to promote her new album and cover over 70 cities. She consistently sold out arenas and had to add extra shows in Japan and all across Europe. Due to her success, in 2001, she signed a new multi-album contract with "Arista Records" for an unprecedented $100 million, making her one of the highest paid entertainers in the world.

Charlie Christian

<u>Major Hall of Fame Inductions</u>

Rock & Roll Hall of Fame
Jazz Hall of Fame
Oklahoma Jazz Hall of Fame

Considered as the "Father of Bebop," Charlie Christian (1916 - 1942) is the most well known of the early amplified Jazz guitarists. Christian was a key figure in the development of Bebop and Cool Jazz music starting in the early 1940's. The amplification of an acoustic instrument was quite new during the early 20th century. His new sound and approach with this type of acoustic guitar influenced the early Bebop recordings of giants such as Dizzy Gillespie, Charlie Parker, Miles Davis and Thelonious Monk and Jimmy Hendrix. Often described as a trailblazer, his unique style transformed the role of the guitar in popular music. Throughout his legendary career, Christian's style has influenced generations of Jazz guitarists and performers.

Swing and Jazz Guitarist, Charlie Christian was a key figure in the development of Bebop and Cool Jazz. Raised in Oklahoma City, his immediate family were all musically talented, his mother played the piano, while his father sang, played the trumpet and guitar. His father and brothers formed a quartet which included Christian when he was 12 years old. While performing with his family in an Oklahoma City night club, Christian met Lester Young, who was a saxophonist in Count Basie's orchestra. Christian was fascinated by Young's style which helped in shaping his own stylistic development.

After years of playing the electric guitar, Christian began leading his own band at the age of 23, shortly after, he was discovered by talent scout, John Hammond, who stopped in an Oklahoma City club where he was performing. The amplified electric guitar was fairly new at the time and he recognized Christian as a trailblazer who helped in making the Jazz guitar solo a practical reality for the first time. Christian quickly realized the potential of the electric guitar, and developed a style which made the most of the unique properties of the instrument.

Christian then travelled to Los Angeles in order to audition with his electric guitar for "Benny Goodman's Band." This move increased his popularity across the country as he worked tirelessly on legitimizing, revolutionizing, and standardizing the electric guitar as a Jazz instrument. After working nights with Goodman, he would often seek out other jam sessions across the country where he previously performed.

He discovered a club in Harlem named "Minton's," located on New York's West 118th Street. While playing at Minton's, Christian performed with future Jazz legends such as Dizzy Gillespie, Charlie Parker, Thelonious Monk, Miles Davis, and Joe Guy. Christian's style impressed them all so much as he used altered chords with his guitar. He soon became known as the "Genius of the Electric Guitar."

Their jam sessions were the best in the country and often lasted until 4 A.M. each morning, eventually leading Minton's to become the birthplace of the "Bebop Movement." His inventive single-note playing helped popularize the electric guitar as a solo instrument. Throughout his legendary career, he had an immense influence on the development of BeBop.

Staple Singers

Major Awards	Wins
R&B Pioneer Award	1

Major Hall of Fame Inductions

Rock & Roll Hall of Fame
Grammy Lifetime Achievement
Grammy Hall of Fame
Blues Hall of Fame
Gospel Music Hall of Fame

Widely known as "The First Family of Song," and one of the most powerful Vocal groups of 1960's and 1970's, "The Staple Singers" embraced an impressive stylistic diversity while always staying true to their roots in Gospel harmonies. Led by Roebuck "Pops" Staples, the quartet first rose to stardom in the Gospel music community before performing Soul and socially conscious R&B hits for "Stax Records" in the 1960's including "Heavy Makes You Happy (Sha-Na-Boom Boom)" and "I'll Take You There." The group was also one of the great voices of the civil rights movement, as Pops" Staples was close friends with Dr. Martin Luther King Jr. For many artists in the 1960's, it was tough to achieve success in a single genre, as a select few were able to reinvent themselves. The Staples Singers managed to achieve greatness in three separate and distinct genres of music during the four decades of their storied career.

Gospel, Soul and R&B singing group "The Staple Singers," were a major force in music, culture and politics during the 1960's and 1970's. This Gospel family group was formed in 1951 when Roebuck "Pops" Staples, his four children Mavis, Pervis, Yvonne, and Cleotha performed in front of church audiences in Chicago, Illinois. The group's lead vocalist were both Pops and Mavis. In 1956, The group signed with Chicago's "Vee Jay Records," and released their first hit "Uncloudy Day." That set the template for Staples classics to come, opening with Pops trademark guitar sound.

As their music became more popular, their Chicago home became a haven for traveling performers, including Ray Charles, Redd Foxx, and Stevie Wonder who were frequent visitors. The "Queen of Soul," Aretha Franklin, often used the Staples home as a place of refuge during the height of her stardom. Coincidentally, Sam Cooke, Curtis Mayfield, Lou Rawls, and Mahalia Jackson were all neighbors of the Staples family.

In 1968, the group signed with Memphis-based "Stax Records," soon after, they released their next 2 albums, "Soul Folk in Action" and "We'll Get Over." The Staple Singers sounded like no other group, led by Mavis, with her husky, sensual lead voice, contrasting with Pops lighter vocals, followed by the rich vocal harmonies of the other siblings. Although they crossed over to Soul and R&B, their music remained profoundly spiritual. During the civil rights movement, they began singing for social justice while working closely with Dr. Martin Luther King Jr., who would often request to hear Pops song, "Why (Am I Treated So Bad?)."

The Staples Singers went on have several No. 1 hits for Stax Records including, "Heavy Makes You Happy (Sha-Na-Boom Boom)" and "I'll Take You There." When Stax encountered financial problems, Curtis Mayfield signed the group to his "Curtom Records" label and produced their next No. 1 hit "Let's Do It Again." The Staples went on to continued chart success. In 1970, Pervis left the group and was replaced by sister Yvonne.

In 1984, Mavis continued to carry on the family tradition and sing with the group, while also working on her own solo ventures. She signed with Prince's "Paisley Park" label, and sung the title song of his 1990 motion picture "Graffiti Bridge," she also made several solo recordings, including her 1995 album "The Voice.

Marian Anderson

Major Awards   Wins

NAACP Image Award	1
Congressional Gold Medal	1
Presidential Medal of Freedom	1

Major Hall of Fame Inductions

Grammy Lifetime Achievement
Grammy Hall of Fame
National Medal of Arts
Hollywood Walk of Fame
Honored on U.S. Postal Stamp

Marian Anderson (1897 - 1993) was one of the most celebrated singers of the 20th century. Most of her singing career was spent performing in concert venues with major orchestras throughout the United States and Europe. For more than five decades, she became a trailblazer in the struggle for African-American artists to overcome racial injustice in the United States. Along with the aid of President Franklin D. Roosevelt and First Lady Eleanor Roosevelt, Anderson performed a critically acclaimed concert on Easter Sunday, in 1939 on the steps of the Lincoln Memorial in Washington, D.C. to a crowd of more than 75,000 people, and a radio audience in the millions. She continued to break barriers for African-American artists in the United States, notably becoming the first African-American to perform at the Metropolitan Opera in New York City in 1955. She later became an important symbol during the civil rights movement in the 1960's, notably singing at the March on Washington in 1963.

Singer Marian Anderson was one of the most influential, celebrated and critically acclaimed Artist of the 20th century. Growing up in Philadelphia, Pennsylvania, Anderson displayed vocal talent as a child, but her family could not afford to pay for formal training. From the age of 6, she was a member in the choir of the Union Baptist Church, where she sang parts written for alto, tenor, and soprano. The congregation raised funds for her to attend a music school for a year.

She then became a student of world famous voice teacher Giuseppe Boghetti at the age of 19, Boghetti was so impressed by her talent that he gave her free lessons for a year. In 1925, she entered a contest with over 300 competitors to sing with the New York Philharmonic Orchestra. Anderson won first prize and her appearance was a great success.

Although many concert opportunities were closed to her because of her race, Anderson appeared with the Philadelphia Symphony and toured HBCU (Historically Black College and University) college campuses. She made her European debut in Berlin in 1930, and maintained her highly successful multi-city European tours for over 10 years. Still relatively unknown in the United States, she received scholarships to study abroad and appeared before the monarchs of Sweden, Norway, Denmark, and England. Her pure vocal quality, richness of tone, and tremendous range made her, in the opinion of many, the world's greatest singer.

Anderson was the first African-American singer to perform as a member of the Metropolitan Opera in New York City. She also made her New York concert debut at "Town Hall" in 1935, which was a personal goal and triumph, she then began a South American tour. In 1939, however, she attempted to rent concert facilities in Washington, D.C.'s Constitution Hall, and was refused due of her race, the incident sparked widespread outrage and protest from many people, including First Lady Eleanor Roosevelt. Arrangements were made for Anderson to instead appear at the Lincoln Memorial on Easter Sunday in 1939, she drew an audience of 75,000.

Anderson later became an important symbol of grace and beauty during the civil rights movement in the 1960's, she also worked for several years as a delegate to the "United Nations Human Rights Committee" and as a "Goodwill Ambassadress" for the United States Department of State.

Bobby Womack

Major Hall of Fame Inductions

Rock & Roll Hall of Fame
Bluesfest Lifetime Achievement

Bobby Womack (1944 - 2014) was an extraordinary musician, he was richly expressive as a singer/songwriter with a long and distinguished career in R&B and Soul. Like many other Soul performers, Womack began performing Gospel music in a church setting, before moving into the secular field as a singer, composer, and guitarist. Womack was immensely popular among U.S. listeners, while achieving superstardom in Europe as well, where his albums sold millions of copies. Although he was able to shine in the spotlight as a solo singer or behind the scenes as an instrumentalist and songwriter, Womack was a consistent hitmaker. His records represented the best in Soul music, in which he learned from the likes of Sam Cooke, Wilson Pickett, and Sly Stone. Womack's career began before the age 10, he later wrote and performed hits such as "That's the Way I feel About Cha" and "If You Think You're Lonely Now." He also wrote "The Rolling Stones" first U.S. No. 1 hit, "It's All Over Now." His raspy voice was behind some of the most soulful songs ever recorded. Throughout his career that spanned more than six decades, he inspired an entire generation of musical legends, including Jimi Hendrix, among others.

Singer, Songwriter, and Producer Bobby Womack was one of the most highly regarded R&B and Soul performers of the late 20th century. Growing up in Cleveland, Ohio, as one of five brothers, his father, an amateur singer, organized them into a Gospel vocal group called "The Womack Brothers." In 1953, the brothers opened for the Gospel group "The Soul Stirrers" and impressed one of its members, Sam Cooke.

After Cooke transitioned to secular Pop music, he persuaded the Womack's to do the same. The group signed to Cooke's record label under the name "The Valentinos," the quintet, with Bobby as lead vocalist, scored R&B hits such as "Lookin' for a Love" and "It's All Over Now." Sadly, soon after Cooke's murder, the brothers took it extremely hard and disbanded. Womack then pursued a career as a solo artist, he refined his sound, which integrated deeply felt vocals and lean guitar work. In 1967, he toured and recorded with legendary singer Ray Charles.

After completing his tour with Charles, Womack moved to Memphis where he worked at "American Studios," he began playing the guitar and was featured on a few of Aretha Franklin's albums. His work as a songwriter brought attention from music executive Wilson Pickett, who insisted on recording some of Womack's songs. In 1968, he signed with "Minit Records" and recorded his debut solo album "Fly Me to the Moon," which featured the hit single "California Dreamin.'"

In 1971, he switched labels and signed with "United Artists," where he released the album "Communication" which kicked off a string of hit songs that ran through the first half of the decade, including his breakout No. 1 hit "That's the Way I Feel About 'Cha." His 1972 follow-up album "Understanding" spawned him into superstardom. Along with his success, Womack remained a vital force in R&B throughout the decade.

In the 1980's, Womack began producing one of his best-known albums, "The Poet," featuring his signature single, "If You Think You're Lonely Now," which peaked in the Soul charts in 1982. He then returned to work in 1984, releasing the "The Poet II" which featured the single "I Wish He Didn't Trust Me So Much." The album sold even better than its predecessor, selling millions of copies, especially in Europe, bringing him international acclaim as a global musical icon.

Teddy Riley

Major Awards	**Wins**
Grammy Award	1
Soul Train Award	1
NAACP Image Award	1

Major Hall of Fame Inductions

Hollywood Walk of Fame

Singer, Songwriter, Producer and Multi-instrumentalist, Teddy Riley (1967 -) has one of the most intriguing legacies in music, he has more than 1000 music credits to his name. In 1987, the dawn of a brand new genre called the "New Jack Swing" was created by Riley. During this era, Riley composed, produced and wrote hundreds of chart-topping, award-winning hit records for his three R&B groups "Guy," "Blackstreet" and "Wreckx-N-Effect," as well as for other artist including Bobby Brown, Mary J. Blige, Patti LaBelle, Whitney Houston, Jay-Z, Snoop Dogg, "Boys II Men" and many more. In 1991, Riley produced the "Dangerous" album by Michael Jackson, which sold more than 32 million copies worldwide and debuted at No. 1 on the charts for 117 consecutive weeks. This was the most successful New Jack Swing album of all times. Riley also produced songs for Michael Jackson's "Invincible" album in 2001.

Singer, Songwriter and Producer, commonly referred to as the "King of New Jack Swing," Edward Theodore Riley, who is known professionally as Teddy Riley is one of the most successful record producers in the history of music. Growing up in Harlem, New York, Riley was a child prodigy who began playing drums at the age of 3, the guitar and the trumpet at the age of 5, and when he turned 8 years old, he began playing piano for the "Little Flower Baptist Church." He later began playing in bands around New York City. After meeting "Kool and the Gang" group member Royal Bayyan, Riley was introduced to the arts of record production and songwriting.

Recognized as the inventor of the "New Jack Swing," he formed the singing trio "Guy" in the mid-1980's, which included Riley and brothers Aaron Hall and Damion Hall. Guy debuted with a self-titled album on the "Uptown/MCA Records" label. The album hit No. 1 on the charts and featured the hit singles "Groove Me," "Teddy's Jam," and "I Like." The group pioneered Riley's New Jack Swing style of R&B and infused a blend of Hip-Hop beats along with the Gospel vocals from the Hall brothers. In the late 1980's, Riley then formed his second group, "Wreckx-N-Effect," with his brothers, Markell, and Brandon Mitchell.

In 1991, Guy and Wreckx-N-Effect disbanded and Riley formed a third group, "Blackstreet" with members Chauncey Hannibal, Dave Hollister, and Levi Little. The group would go on to release several major hit records, including "Don't Leave Me," "Girlfriend/Boyfriend" and their signature single "No Diggity." After spearheading these three groups, Riley then applied himself vigorously to a number of new projects. He fused Hip-Hop and R&B in his production work with artists such as Michael Jackson, Stevie Wonder Mary J. Blige and Bobby Brown.

Dubbed "the single most influential producer in music," Riley achieved prominence as he significantly shaped the new sound of R&B. Making a natural progression into motion pictures, Riley hit the big screen with film credits such as, "Do the Right Thing," "House Party," "Money Train," "Panther," "Get on the Bus" and "Preacher's Wife." He is also the first African-American music producer from the U.S. to produce K-Pop (Korean Pop Music) and bring it to America. Worldwide, Riley has produced hundreds of artists and has countless music credits to his name.

Elizabeth T. Greenfield

Often referred to as "The Black Swan" due to her sweet tones and wide vocal compass, internationally hailed performer, Elizabeth T. Greenfield (1824 - 1876) became the Nation's first African-American Concert singer, in many ways she was the first Pop star in the United States. Greenfield toured the United States, Canada and Europe extensively during her career, she was the best known African-American concert performer in the 19th century. In 1853, she also became the first African-American woman to give a command performance before royalty when she appeared before Queen Victoria of England. Greenfield inspired an entire generation and the paved the way for a host of female concert singers. In 1921, entrepreneur, musician and music publisher, Harry Pace successfully opened the first African-American owned record company in the world in Massachusetts, he named the company "Black Swan Records," in her honor.

Singer and Songwriter, who was considered as the best-known African-American concert performer of the 19th century, Elizabeth Taylor Greenfield was in many ways the Nation's first Pop star. Born into slavery in 1824, she was raised in Natchez, Mississippi, Greenfield had little reason to dream of the life that would eventually become her own. As a child, she was taken to Philadelphia, Pennsylvania by a Quaker family who believed in freedom and provided her with a new beginning.

Growing up as a teenager in Philadelphia, Greenfield discovered a love for music, as a self-taught singer, she supported herself by giving public and private performances. She soon gained recognition throughout the Northeast for her performances, she was affectionately dubbed as "The Black Swan" due to her sweet tones and rich vocal harmonies. In 1852, Greenfield made her debut at Metropolitan Hall in New York City, (one of the largest performance halls in the world) performing in front of more than 4,000 patrons.

As her reputation grew as a concert singer, she toured the United States and Canada extensively. Six months after her New York City Premier, she began a European tour, she performed in Scotland, Ireland and England. While in London, she met the Royal Family's organist, George Smart and was invited to perform for the Queen. In 1853, Greenfield gave a command performance of a lifetime for Queen Victoria at Buckingham Palace, making her the first African-American singer to perform before British Royalty. Best known for her performances of opera and classical music, she became a global iconic figure.

As an abolitionist, Greenfield was also a strong supporter of African-Americans being free and having equal rights. After returning from her European tour, America was experiencing a civil war, Greenfield appeared alongside leaders such as Frederick Douglass and Frances E.W. Harper to give speeches as well as perform. While traveling and performing throughout the country, she raised funds for various causes such as anti-slavery and abolitionist movements.

Greenfield possessed a natural voice of great purity and extraordinary power, her legacy as a world renown singer has paved the way for countless generations of African-American female concert singers.

Barry White

Major Awards   **Wins**

Major Awards	Wins
Grammy Awards	2
American Music Awards	9
Soul Train Music Awards	5

Major Hall of Fame Inductions

Dance Music Hall of Fame
Hollywood Walk of Fame

Singer and Composer, Barry White (1944 - 2003) was known as the undisputed "Maestro of Sensual Soul music," due to his growling seductive lyrics in a deep, husky voice backed by lush orchestration. He was a prolific songwriter who produced a string of hit songs such as "Can't Get Enough of Your Love, Babe" and "You're the First, the Last, My Everything." White bridged the gap between Soul and Disco and provided a soundtrack for seduction in the 1970's. He had the ability to build lush arrangements and catchy melodies around his grooves. Along with the combination of his bass-baritone voice as well as his sensuous delivery, White's recordings were irresistible to all of his many fans. Over the course of his legendary career that spanned more than three decades, White has sold over 100 million records worldwide, making him one of the world's best-selling artists of all time.

Singer, Songwriter, Producer and Composer, often referred to as "The Maestro," Barry White grew up singing Gospel songs with his mother in church while teaching himself how to play the piano and master various other instruments. He made his recording debut at the tender age of 11, playing piano on singer, Jesse Belvin's 1956 Doo-wop hit "Goodnight My Love." He then made his first record at the age of 16 with a group called "The Upfronts," they recorded the single "Little Girl."

As a young man, White served as a producer for a number of other minor bands. He helped launch a female R&B group called "Love Unlimited" in the early 1970's, he wrote and arranged their classic Soul hit ballad "Walking in the Rain With the One I Love" (1972). He then wrote several other songs and recorded them while deciding pursue his own solo career.

The result was the smooth, deep voiced White producing his first solo album, "I've Got So Much to Give" (1973). The album included the title track and his first solo chart hit, "I'm Gonna Love You Just a Little More Baby," which also rose to No. 1 on the Billboard R&B charts. A string of hit singles followed with White's debut album over the next few years, including, "Never, Never Gonna Give You Up," "Can't Get Enough of Your Love, Babe," and "It's Ecstasy When You Lay Down Next to Me."

Although the Disco era came to an end during the late 1970's, White maintained a loyal following throughout his career, in 1979, he founded his own recording company, "Unlimited Gold." During the 1990's, he enjoy a renewed wave of popularity after participating in the song "The Secret Garden (Sweet Seduction Suite)" from Quincy Jones 1989 album, "Back on the Block," White then mounted an effective comeback with several albums. He then released a series of commercially successful albums that proved his status as an elite performer, each album was more successful than the last.

During the course of his career in the music business which spanned more than three decades, White has garnered an astounding 106 gold albums, 41 of which attained platinum status. Along with his worldwide record sales in excess of 100 million sold, he is one of the best-selling recording artists in history.

169

Wynton Marsalis

Major Awards	Wins
Grammy Awards	9
Porin Award	1
Pulitzer Prize for Music	1
Emmy Award	1
NAACP Image Award	1
Soul Train Music Award	1

Major Hall of Fame Inductions

National Medal of Arts
National Humanities Medal

Widely regarded as one of the greatest Jazz musicians of all time, World-renowned Trumpeter and Composer, Wynton Marsalis (1961 -) began his classical training on the trumpet at the age of 12, he then entered "The Juilliard School" at the age 17, before joining the group "The Jazz Messengers." He made his recording debut in 1982, and has since released more than 60 Classical and Jazz recordings. In 1983, he became the first and only artist in history to win both Classical and Jazz Grammy Awards in the same year and repeated this feat in 1984. He also co-founded "Jazz at Lincoln Center" which hosts up to 500 events annually. Marsalis has been named by both Time and Life Magazines as one of America's most influential people. In 2001, he was appointed as a United Nations "Messenger of Peace."

Trumpeter, Composer and Bandleader, Wynton Marsalis emerged as
one of the greatest Jazz musicians in history. Growing up in New Orleans,
Louisiana, he was part of a great musical family. Considered the "First Family
of Jazz," his father Ellis Marsalis Jr. (pianist and music teacher) along with
brothers Jason, Delfeayo, and Branford all had a major impact on Jazz in
the late 20th and early 21st centuries.

Marsalis exhibited a passion for music at an early age, by the age of 8, he
was already performing traditional New Orleans music in his local church
band. Four years later he began studying the trumpet and soon performed
in local Jazz and Funk bands. When he turned 14 years old, he performed
with the New Orleans Philharmonic. Marsalis became devoted to Jazz while
studying at "The Berkshire Music Center." In 1979, he moved to New York
City and attended "The Juilliard School," he was soon recognized as one of
the most gifted musicians at the institution.

His arrival to New York inspired a new age of trumpet players and launched
a new era called "The Young Lions Movement in Jazz," resulting in major
record labels signing and promoting young Jazz musicians. He championed
for older and overlooked Jazz musicians of the past and helped to promote
a resurgence of the genre. The Jazz renaissance that followed was largely
credited to him and brother Branford's influence.

In 1983, a year after making his recording debut, Marsalis became the first
and only artist to win both Classical and Jazz Grammy Awards in the same
year, an accomplishment he repeated in 1984. Since that time, he has
recorded more than 60 Jazz and Classical albums. He is the only artist in
any genre to have won Grammy Awards for 5 consecutive years (1983 - 1987)
and the first Jazz artist to be awarded the Pulitzer Prize in Music. In 1987, he
helped launch the "Classical Jazz Summer Concert Series" at Lincoln Center
in New York City. The success of that series led to the creation of "Jazz at
Lincoln Center," of which Marsalis serves as Artistic and Musical Director.

Since he developed his own distinctive style in the 1980's, he consistently
ranked among the all-time great Jazz trumpeters, playing everything
from New Orleans Jazz to hard Bop. Throughout his legendary career,
he became a prominent spokesman for Jazz and music education.

Dinah Washington

Major Awards   **Wins**

Grammy Award   1

Major Hall of Fame Inductions

Rock & Roll Hall of Fame
Grammy Hall of Fame
Alabama Jazz Hall of Fame
Big Band and Jazz Hall of Fame
Honored on U.S. Postal Stamp

Known as "The Queen of the Blues," Dinah Washington (1924 - 1963) was one of the most beloved, versatile, and popular singers of the 1950's. As an artistic descendent of Classic Blues Divas such as Bessie Smith and Ma Rainey, she built on her early Gospel roots to master a wide range of genres, including Jazz, Blues, and R&B. Noted for her excellent voice control and unique Gospel-influenced delivery, Washington became known as the best Jazz and Blues singer of her era, she ascended to Pop superstardom with several hit songs including, "What a Difference a Day Makes," "Unforgettable," "This Bitter Earth," "September in the Rain," and "Where Are You?" In 2008, the city of Tuscaloosa, Alabama (Washington's birthplace), renamed the section of 30th Avenue between 15th Street and Kaulton Park "Dinah Washington Avenue," in honor of her legendary career.

Singer and Pianist, who is often referred to as "The Queen of the Blues," Ruth Lee Jones, professionally known as Dinah Washington was one of the most popular African-American recording artists of the 1950's. Born in Tuscaloosa, Alabama, Washington and her family moved to Chicago, Illinois when she was 4 years old. While growing up, she was taught how to play piano and sing by her mother. Soon after, she joined her mother in the choir, by the age of 11, she was performing as a Gospel vocalist in church recitals across the country.

When Washington turned 15 years old, she won an amateur talent contest at a Chicago theater, soon after, she began performing in nightclubs as a Jazz pianist and vocalist. In 1943, talent agent Joe Glaser told renowned bandleader Lionel Hampton about Washington and her remarkable voice. An impressed Hampton asked her to sing with his orchestra at Chicago's Regal Theater. Following that guest performance, she was hired by Hampton and he gave her the stage name Dinah Washington.

Washington earned acclaim for her live singing due to her performances eclipsing anyone who followed her. She remained with Hampton's band until 1946, she then decided to pursue a solo career. After signing with "Mercury Records" she recorded one of her signature anthems "Slick Chick (On The Mellow Side)" and was billed as "The Queen of the Blues." During the 1950's, Washington recorded with some of the most acclaimed Jazz musicians of the era, including drummer, Jimmy Cobb and saxophonist, Julian "Cannonball" Adderly.

In 1955, she recorded the album, "For Those in Love," which was arranged by producer Quincy Jones. The Jazz-based album included the singles, "This Can't Be Love," "I Could Write a Book" and "You Don't Know What Love Is." Washington's exceptional talent and range made her a "cross-over superstar," her insistence on singing and recording what she liked, regardless of genre conventions, made her an icon of personal vision and artistic integrity.

In 2013, the city of Tuscaloosa dedicated "The Dinah Washington Cultural Arts Center," in her honor to highlight her career and life. She was also honored by the city of Chicago in 2005, when the Board of Commissioners renamed a park, (near where she lived) "The Dinah Washington Park."

New Edition

Major Awards   **Wins**

American Music Awards   2
Soul Train Music Awards   2

Major Hall of Fame Inductions

BET Lifetime Achievement
Soul Train Lifetime Achievement
Hollywood Walk of Fame

Vocal group, "New Edition" has mesmerized audiences with their signature choreographed shows, smooth vocal harmonies and electrifying showmanship cementing their place in history as one of the most successful groups ever. The group has remained an unstoppable measurement of true R&B, Hip-Hop and Pop music. In 1983, the New Edition phenomenon began in Boston, Massachusetts, with teenagers Ronnie DeVoe, Bobby Brown, Ricky Bell, Michael Bivins, and Ralph Tresvant. In 1986, Bobby Brown left the group to begin a highly-charged solo career, soon after solo artist, Johnny Gill joined the band. In 1989, they orchestrated one of music's biggest coups by simultaneously launching Ralph Tresvant and Johnny Gill's solo albums, while Ricky Bell, Michael Bivins and Ronnie DeVoe created the high-octane group, "Bell-Biv-DeVoe," which spawned the cross-over hit record, "Poison." Between their various projects, they sold a cumulative 30 million records worldwide, altogether they have dominated the Billboard charts for over three decades.

Vocal Group, "New Edition" was the most popular teen heartthrob group of the 1980's, as they matured and progressed, they laid much of the groundwork for the fusion of Hip-Hop and R&B through their music. Formed in the Roxbury section of Boston, Massachusetts, by Ricky Bell, Michael Bivins, and Bobby Brown, they began singing together in 1978 while still in elementary school, they later recruited neighborhood friends Ralph Tresvant Ronnie DeVoe.

Discovered by writer and producer, Maurice Starr, who signed the group to his "Streetwise Records" label in hopes of launching a "Jackson 5" phenomenon for the 1980's. The group's members ages ranged from 13 to 15 when they released their first hit single, "Candy Girl" in 1983, which was a chart-topping R&B hit. Their debut album, also titled, Candy Girl, spawned 2 more hit singles, "Popcorn Love" and "Is This the End." The group was then offered a deal by a major label, "MCA Records."

In 1985, New Edition had reached full-fledged teen idol status with the release of their No. 1 hit singles, "Cool It Now," and "Mr. Telephone Man." As they released their next album, "All for Love," they continued growing up fast, their voices began changing and their material was becoming more adult, with harder-edged Funk and more mature romantic ballads. In 1986, Brown decided to leave the group in order pursue a solo career, he was then replaced by singer, Johnny Gill, a deep-voiced friend of the group who was already recording as a solo artist. Gill made his debut on the 1989 album, "Heart Break," which found New Edition working with producers, Jimmy Jam and Terry Lewis. The group scored several R&B hits from the album, including "Can You Stand the Rain."

After the success of the Heart Break album, the group decided to split up and work on separate projects, Brown had already become a superstar after the release of his album, "Don't Be Cruel." Gill returned to his solo career and scored major hit records, and Tresvant also went solo. The remainder of the group teamed up as "Bell Biv DeVoe" and had massive success with their debut album, "Poison," Bivins also managed and helped produce a new talented young group, "Boyz II Men." In 1996, New Edition announced its triumphant reunion, with all six members participating in an R&B supergroup. They released the album, "Home Again," it debuted at No. 1, with chart-topping singles, "Hit Me Off," and "Still in Love with You."

Chubby Checker

Major Awards	Wins
Grammy Award	1
R&B Pioneer Award	1
Guinness World Record	1

Major Hall of Fame Inductions

Grammy Hall of Fame

Deemed as one of the Pop cultural symbols of the early 1960's, Chubby Checker (1941 -) was the unrivaled "King of the Rock & Roll Dance Craze." Most of the his hit records promoted dancing along \with the song, including "The Pony," "The Fly," and "The Hucklebuck." In 1960, he released his signature recording of "The Twist," the song remains the first and only single to reached No. 1 on the Pop charts twice, in 1960 and 1962. When Checker promoted a dance by the same title, he made musical history and set off one of the greatest dance crazes of the 20th century. The song also popularized a new style of couples dancing that continues to be influential to this day.

Singer, Actor and Dancer, widely known for popularizing many dance styles, Ernest Evans, professionally known as Chubby Checker is synonymous with igniting the greatest dance crazes of the 20th century. As a teenager growing up in Philadelphia, Pennsylvania, he was well known in his neighborhood for his accurate impressions of singers Fats Domino and Jerry Lee Lewis.

Performing at work, in church, and on the streets by night along with his harmonizing group, "The Quantrells," he was given the nickname "Chubby" due to his portly build, soon after he was offered a recording contract by "Cameo Records." In 1960, Checker's first two hit singles for Cameo included "The Class" and "Dancing Dinosaur," followed by his next single titled, "The Twist," which gave birth to the "Twist Dance Craze" which exploded nationwide.

Cameo Records was located in Philadelphia, which was also home to Dick Clark's nationally televised dance show "American Bandstand." Checker landed an appearance on the popular program, ensuring a wide audience for his catchy songs and dance routines. He earned the surname "Checker" from Clark's wife, who likened the singer to Fats Domino. As a dance movement, "The Twist" revolutionized popular culture by giving couples the freedom to break apart on the dance floor. Teenagers and adults began to request the song in nightclubs across the country, due to the dance itself being so simple to perform on the dance floor.

In 1960, "The Twist" became a massive hit, reaching No. 1 for a total of 40 weeks and setting a record as the only song to reach No. 1 twice (again in 1962). Checker followed his hit song with a succession of similar songs, including "Twistin USA," "Let's Twist Again," "Twist It Up," and "Slow Twistin," he had 6 Top-10 hits between 1961 and 1963. He also inspired more dance crazes with other singles such as "The Hucklebuck," "The Pony," "The Fly," "The Slop," and "The Limbo."

In 2012, Checker set a new Guinness World Record in DeLand, Florida, when he sang the Twist song live in front of a dancing crowd. An estimated 4,000 people twisted along with Checker surpassing the previous record for people performing the twist dance at once.

Lionel Hampton

Major Hall of Fame Inductions

Alabama Jazz Hall of Fame
National Medal of Arts

Lionel Hampton (1908 - 2002) is one of the most extraordinary musicians of the 20th century, his artistic achievements symbolize the impact that Jazz music continues to have on our culture in the 21st century. As a bandleader, he established the "Lionel Hampton Orchestra," which became known around the world for its tremendous energy and dazzling showmanship. His signature tunes "Sunny Side of the Street," "Central Avenue Breakdown," "Flying Home," and "Hamp's Boogie-Woogie" all became chart-topping best-sellers upon release. His name became world famous overnight, and his orchestra had a phenomenal array of sidemen. The band also initiated the first phase of Hampton's career as an educator by graduating such talents as Quincy Jones, Dinah Washington, and Aretha Franklin. He was also asked by President Eisenhower to serve as a Goodwill Ambassador for the United States, in which his band made many tours to Europe, Africa and the Middle East, generating a huge international following.

Jazz Vibraphonist, Pianist, and Singer, Lionel Hampton was one of the most popular and exciting Jazz bandleaders of the 1940's and 1950's. Growing up in Birmingham, Alabama, he received his first musical training as a drummer at the age of 15. He later relocated with his family to Chicago, Illinois, where he attended St. Monica's High School. Hampton began his career as a drummer in the "Les Hite Band." The band relocated to Los Angeles, California in the late 1920's and became a regular attraction during their residency at the city's "Cotton Club."

During a 1930 recording session at NBC studios in Los Angeles, Louis Armstrong and Hampton teamed up to record a Jazz album, featuring Hampton on the vibraphone (which would become his signature instrument). In 1934, he then joined the "Benny Goodman Orchestra" which became one of the first integrated Jazz bands in the country. In 1941, Hampton left Goodman to form his own band called the "Lionel Hampton Orchestra."

His Orchestra attracted a wide array of rising Jazz stars including, Quincy Jones, Dinah Washington, Aretha Franklin and Joe Williams among others. Hampton's Orchestra during the 1940's and early 1950's ranked with the Duke Ellington and Count Basie Orchestras as one of the leading bands in the world. He attracted a new international audience when his orchestra began touring Europe, Africa, Asia and the Middle East.

As a composer and arranger, Hampton wrote more than 200 compositions, including the Jazz standards "Flying Home," "Evil Gal Blues," and "Midnight Sun." He was also a successful businessman, establishing two record labels, his own publishing company, and was the founder of the Lionel Hampton Development Corporation, which built low-income housing in inner cities across the country.

Known as an educator of Jazz, he began working with the University of Idaho in the early 1980's to establish his dream of expanding music education nationwide. In 1985, the University named in his honor, "The Lionel Hampton International Jazz Festival," "The Lionel Hampton School of Music," and the "International Jazz Collections Archives," which are located in the University's Library. All were designed to help teach students and preserve the heritage of Jazz music.

Janet Jackson

Major Awards	Wins
Grammy Awards	5
American Music Awards	11
Billboard Music Awards	11
MTV Video Music Awards	9
Guinness World Records	9
Soul Train Music Awards	13
NAACP Image Awards	3

Major Hall of Fame Inductions

Rock & Roll Hall of Fame
Music & Dance Hall of Fame
Hollywood Walk of Fame

Born into one of the most successful musical families in the history of Popular music, Janet Jackson (1966 -) began her entertainment career first as a television actress, she then established herself as a musical talent by the end of the 1980's. At the tender age of 16, she released her debut album, shortly after she began to score large-scale hit records, soon rivaling the astonishing success of her superstar brother Michael Jackson. She has not only released a number of smash singles during her career that has spanned more than four decades, but she has also sold over 100 million records worldwide, Jackson is ranked as one of the best-selling artists in the history of contemporary music.

Singer, Songwriter, Actress and Dancer, who has evolved into a Global Icon, Janet Jackson has emerged from the shadows of her famous brothers to become a megastar in her own right, as well as one of the best-selling artist of the 20th century. Growing up as the youngest of 9 children to Joseph and Katherine Jackson in Gary, Indiana, her older brothers had already begun performing together as "The Jackson 5" by the time she was born.

In 1977, she began a sitcom acting career at the age of 10, she was selected to join the cast of the 1970's hit show "Good Times," as the lovable character "Penny." While continuing acting throughout her teenage years, she was encouraged by her father / manager, Joseph to launch a singing career. They both hired her a new manager, John McClain, who wanted her to also train as a dancer. McClain then introduced Jackson to producers / writers, Jimmy Jam and Terry Lewis, whom she previously saw performing as members of the Minneapolis Funk group "The Time."

Jackson collaborated with Jam and Lewis on most of the tracks for her album, "Control," which presented her as a confident and tough-minded artist (with a soft side and a sense of humor) taking charge of her life for the first time. Control became an instant hit record, along with several singles which topped the Billboard charts including, "What Have You Done for Me Lately," "When I Think of You," "Nasty" and "Let's Wait Awhile." The album sold 5 million copies worldwide, establishing her as a Pop star.

In 1991, she signed the first of two record-breaking, multi-million dollar recording contracts with Virgin Records, which established her as one of the highest paid artists in the music industry. By the end of the 1990's, she was named the most successful recording artist of the decade. Her albums "Janet" and "All for You," were massive hits, both reaching No. 1 on the Billboard charts.

While recording albums and selling out record breaking concerts on her world tours, Jackson relaunched her acting career appearing in several motion pictures, including a couple of movie franchises such as "The Nutty Professor" and "Why did I get Married." Her longevity and achievements reflect her influence in shaping and redefining the scope of popular music. She has also been cited as an inspiration by several iconic performers.

The Spinners

Major Hall of Fame Inductions

Grammy Lifetime Achievement
Grammy Hall of Fame
National Medal of Arts
Vocal Group Hall of Fame
Hollywood Walk of Fame

R&B and Soul Vocal group, "The Spinners" emerged as one of the greatest groups from the 1960's and 1970's. Established in Detroit, Michigan, the five founding members (who all met in high school) were Billy Henderson, Edgar Edwards, Bobby Smith, Henry Fambrough, and Pervis Jackson. Throughout their legendary career that has spanned more than six decades, they released classic timeless hits such as "I'll Be Around," "Working My Way Back to You," "Could It Be I'm Falling in Love," "Mighty Love," "Then Came You," "Games People Play" and "Rubberband Man." Their amazing vocal ability and great stage presence are what set them apart from many groups of their era. They stood the test of time and fought for their place in the music industry, which is not something all groups can say. They wanted to spread good vibes to their fans, which is exactly what they did and continue to do for anyone who listens to their music today. Their songs are staples in many African-American communities and households throughout the country.

Vocal Group, "The Spinners" have created a body of work that has defined the lush, seductive sound of "Philly Soul" for over six decades. The group was formed in 1955 in Detroit, Michigan, and consisted of five members (throughout the group's history specific members varied). The original five members were Billy Henderson, Edgar Edwards, Bobby Smith, Henry Fambrough, and Pervis Jackson.

Originally called the "Domingoes," this group of high school friends formed a unique sound. After a couple years of performing together in Detroit, producer, Harvey Fuqua signed them to his label, "Tri Phi Records" in 1961. Their first single "That's What Girls are Made For" was released that very same year. The song was an instant summer hit and peaked to the Top-10 of R&B hits, it was followed by their next hit song, "Love (I'm So Glad) I Found You." The release of these records began to give the group some real traction in the music industry.

In 1963, "Motown Records" bought out Tri Phi Records, thus making The Spinners official Motown artists. For the next several years, the group was not releasing any new hit records due to not receiving the necessary attention from Motown, who was more focused on the success of "The Temptations," "The Four Tops," and "The Supremes." Atlantic Records recording artist known as "The Queen of Soul," Aretha Franklin suggested the group finish their Motown contract and sign with "Atlantic Records."

In 1970, they left Motown and signed with Atlantic Records and began working with producer Thom Bell, who gave the group a new lush, seductive sound known as "Philly Soul." The Spinners instantly began topping the R&B and Pop charts with the release of some of their classic hits such as "I'll Be Around," "Working My Way Back to You," "Could It Be I'm Falling in Love," "Mighty Love," "Then Came You," "Games People Play" and "Rubberband Man."

While they have sold millions of records, their success at Atlantic Records consistently grew each year. They continued to release timeless music, perform onstage, and earn the respect they missed at Motown. Known for their career longevity, the group has acquired 12 consecutive gold records with their hits climbing to the top of both the Pop and R&B charts, they are also one of the few groups in music history who has had 4 lead singers.

Solomon Burke

Major Awards   **Wins**

Major Awards	Wins
Grammy Award	1
R&B Pioneer Award	1

Major Hall of Fame Inductions

Rock & Roll Hall of Fame

Known as the "King of Rock and Soul," Solomon Burke (1940 - 2010) was a minister and renowned singer of Gospel, R&B and Soul music, with a career spanning over seven decades. Credited with coining the term "Soul music," he is heralded as one of one of the best Soul singers of all time. Beginning his career as a Gospel singer and preacher in the 1960's, he made the transition to R&B (similar to Aretha Franklin and Wilson Pickett) and signed with "Atlantic Records," focusing his career on secular music. He had a string of R&B hits, including "Cry to Me," "If You Need Me (Call Me)," "Tonight's the Night," and "Goodbye Baby (Baby Goodbye)." Burke's music was world renown, he was invited to the Vatican several times to perform for both Pope John Paul II and Pope Benedict XVI for the Vatican's Christmas celebration. His highly polished, emotional songs set the pattern for successful, early Soul music. Burke's music played a major role in influencing major artists like "The Rolling Stones," who on their early albums covered Burke's "Cry to Me" and "Everybody Needs Somebody to Love."

Gospel, R&B and Soul Singer, often referred to as the "King of Rock and Soul," Solomon Burke is one of the founding fathers of "Soul music." Growing up in Philadelphia, Pennsylvania, Burke was greatly involved in his faith, which gave him inspiration for his musical career. In 1947, at the age of 7, he gave his first sermon, by the age of 12, he was a minister who was called the "Wonder Boy Preacher." When he turned 21 years old, he was an ordained Bishop of his Philadelphia church.

In 1954, Burke's music career began after his musical talent was scouted by a local Philadelphia DJ, who brought him to a recording studio in New York City, where he produced his first hit record, "Christmas Presents from Heaven." In 1961, Burke then signed with "Atlantic Records" and began to bring out several hit songs such as "Down in the Valley," and "Cry to Me."

In 1964, he wrote and recorded his signature single, "Everybody Needs Somebody to Love." The song was almost immediately covered by "The Rolling Stones" and later by Wilson Pickett, who paid tribute to Burke in his preaching-style introduction to the song. While at Atlantic Records, under producer Bert Berns, Burke became one of the first R&B performers to be called a Soul singer, based on the success of his songs "Cry to Me," "If You Need Me (Call Me)," "Goodbye Baby (Baby Goodbye)," "Got to Get You off My Mind," and "Tonight's the Night."

Burke was one of the chief architects of classic Soul music, he produced albums in a style that merged his Gospel and R&B roots. As a result, his music was mainly marketed to an audience that appreciated his musical roots. His live and recorded music remained a favorite of those who wanted to experience a legendary Soul singer who maintained his original style.

Over the next six decades, Burke would have a prolific music career, releasing 18 albums, selling more than 17 million records, and touring worldwide to perform before lovers of Soul music. Burke was also credited with coining the term "Soul Music." Outside of his music career, he was active as a member of his church community in his "House of Prayer for All People." He remained the leader of the congregation for over 60 years.

185

The Platters

Major Awards   **Wins**

NME Award for World Group   1

Major Hall of Fame Inductions

Rock & Roll Hall of Fame
Grammy Hall of Fame
Vocal Group Hall of Fame

Vocal R&B group, "The Platters" were one of the most successful groups during the Rock & Roll era. The original band consisted of Alex Hodge, Cornell Gunter, David Lynch, Joe Jefferson, Gaynel Hodge, and a late addition, Herb Reed, who joined after being discharged from the Army in 1953. After joining "Mercury Records," they released several chart-topping singles including, "Only You," "The Great Pretender," "(You've Got) The Magic Touch," "He's Mine" and "Enchanted." The Platters holds the unique distinction as the first Rock & Roll group to have an album reach the Top-10 on Pop charts in the United States. Throughout their legendary career that has spanned over six decades, the group has recorded nearly 400 songs and sold over 80 million records worldwide. The Platters have also appeared in 27 motion pictures such as "Rock Around The Clock," "Girl's Town," and "Europe By Night."

Vocal R&B group "The Platters" were one of the most successful groups in the world during the 20th century. Formed in Los Angeles, California, in 1954, the band consisted of Alex Hodge, Cornell Gunter, Joe Jefferson, Gaynel Hodge, and Army Veteran, Herb Reed. Their name was derived from the metal disk, or "platters," that rotate vinyl records and on the turntable.

Shortly after the original group was formed, Jefferson, Gunther and Hodge dropped out, and were immediately replaced by Tony Williams, David Lynch, and Paul Robi. Zola Taylor also joined the group and became the first female vocalist to break through the gender divide as part of an all-male vocal group. This second lineup of the newly formed quintet is often mistakenly referred to as the "Original Platters." The group's humble beginnings were soon turned around when they were introduced to music producer, acclaimed songwriter and manager, Samuel "Buck" Ram, they were then signed to a major deal with "Mercury Records."

In 1955, The Platters released their first hit single, "Only You," which became an instant hit and would eventually reach No. 1 on the Pop charts, pioneering the "new sound" of Rock & Roll. Their follow-up single, "The Great Pretender," topped the charts once again and provided the launch pad for their rise as crossover artists. As a result, The Platters became the first African-American group to achieve international superstardom.

Considered the most romantic of all the Doo-wop groups during the time, they charted several No. 1 hits during the 1950's and 1960's including "(You've Got) The Magic Touch," "He's Mine" and "Enchanted." Their songs were extremely popular at parties when slow dance records were played. Lead vocalist, Tony Williams had been trained by singing in church Gospel groups, which contributed to his deep and clear vocals.

The Platters unique vocal style had touched a nerve in the music-buying public, selling over 80 million records worldwide. They became an international sensation, touring the world in the 1960's and were dubbed by Mercury Records as "International Ambassadors of Goodwill." The group's single "Out of My Mind," sold over one million copies alone and was the considered one of the first song ever to have a music video.

Eartha Kitt

Major Awards   **Wins**

Emmy Awards   3
Annie Awards   3

Major Hall of Fame Inductions

Hollywood Walk of Fame

Eartha Kitt (1927 - 2008) was an international star who gave new meaning to the word versatile. She distinguished herself in music, theater, film, and television. Her Broadway stardom led to a recording contract and a succession of best-selling records including "St. Louis Blues," "Just an Old Fashioned Girl, "A Woman Wouldn't Be," and her signature hit Christmas song, "Santa Baby." Singing in 10 different languages and performing in over 100 countries, her legendary career has spanned over five decades. As an award-winning actress, Kitt made her mark on Pop culture with her groundbreaking role as the infamous "Catwoman" in the popular 1960's television series, "Batman." She immediately became synonymous with the role and her trademark growl became a global phenomenon. Kitt was one of the first African-American icons in the entertainment world.

Singer, Actress, and Activist, Eartha Mae Keith, better known as Eartha Kitt was known for her sultry vocals and success as a stage and film actress. Growing up in Harlem, New York City, she joined "Katherine Dunham's Dance Troupe" at the age of 16, she then began touring the United States, Mexico, South America, and Europe. When the Dunham company returned to the U.S., the multi-lingual Kitt stayed in Paris, where she won immediate popularity as a nightclub singer and actress. She entertained audiences from across the world with her provocative dancing and singing.

Kitt's blend of sensuality and sophistication made her an instant hit with international audiences. She drew critical acclaim which established her as a serious actress, starring in two French films before returning home to New York and appearing on Broadway in 1952. By the mid-1950's, she prevailed as a variety artist, and it was apparent that she was destined for superstardom, she then signed with "RCA Records" and began her recording career.

Kitt was able to sing in 10 different languages, her best-selling records included "St. Louis Blues," "Just an Old Fashioned Girl, "A Woman Wouldn't Be," and her signature hit Christmas song, "Santa Baby." Her singing style would later be the template for other singers with pillow-talk voices like Diana Ross (who said she patterned her Supremes sound and look largely after Kitt). During her performances, her voice "purred" and she would prowl across the stage "flashing her claws similar to a kitten." Appropriately she was tapped to play "Catwoman" in the popular 1960's television series "Batman."

Known as the "most exciting woman in the world," Kitt also starred in several theater and motion picture roles during the 1960's including being casted as "Helen of Troy" in the stage production of "Faust," and earning an Academy Award nomination for her role in "Anna Lucasta."

Along with her legendary career that has spanned over 50 years, Kitt has performed in music, theater, television and motion pictures in over 100 countries. As a staunch civil rights activist, she was outspoken on her opposition for the war in Vietnam. As a philanthropist, much of the proceeds from her concerts assisted in helping the homeless and building schools for African-American children across the country.

John Coltrane

Major Awards   **Wins**

Grammy Award   1
Porin Award   1
Pulitzer Prize for Music   1

Major Hall of Fame Inductions

Grammy Lifetime Achievement
Grammy Hall of Fame
Honored on U.S. Postal Stamp

John Coltrane (1926 - 1967) emerged as one of the most innovative and influential Jazz musicians of the 20th century. As a revolutionary and groundbreaking Jazz saxophonist, he was an iconic figure who worked alongside famed musicians and bandleaders such as Dizzy Gillespie, Duke Ellington and Miles Davis. Coltrane turned the Jazz world upside down with his outstanding and ingenious saxophone play, he nurtured a distinctive sound defined in part by an ability to play several notes at once. He became a global iconic figure with albums such as "Giant Steps," "My Favorite Things" and "A Love Supreme." Coltrane had an immense impact on the music world, he revolutionized Jazz with his demanding techniques while showing a deep reverence for sounds from other countries, which included Latin America, South Asia and several African Nations. In 2007, he was also posthumously awarded the Pulitzer Prize for music.

Jazz Saxophonist, Bandleader and Composer, John Coltrane is recognized as a global iconic figure in the world of Jazz music and one of the most influential Jazz musicians of the 20th century. Growing up in High Point, North Carolina, he was influenced by religion and spirituality beginning in childhood, his grandfather was a minister at an AME church. In 1943, he moved to Philadelphia and enrolled in "The Ornstein School of Music."

Coltrane's musical education was interrupted when he was drafted into the U.S. Navy during World War II. While serving, he discovered his love of Jazz music while performing with a Hawaii-based Naval band. After leaving the Navy in 1945, he made his professional debut as an artist. He worked for a number of bandleaders including Dizzy Gillespie and Earl Bostic. As his reputation grew, he began working with some of the most famous Jazz artists of the era. Between 1955 and 1959, he played in a band led by the legendary trumpeter Miles Davis, and also worked with famed Jazz pianist Thelonious Monk.

In 1958, Coltrane formed his own band which eventually became known as "The Classic Quartet," he practiced a unique compositional and improvisational technique that he developed based on his saxophone playing. He quickly emerged as the leading Jazz tenor saxophonist of the era, and often referred to as the "High Priest" of avant-garde Jazz. Coltrane's style involved dense, rapidly changing chords with complex extensions built upon each note. Rejecting traditional harmonies, his quartet soon became a platform for introducing new ideas into Jazz.

Coltrane's innovative style was evident on his 1959 album, "Giant Steps," which remains a marker of musical excellence. He incorporated African music and the Blues into his compositions as well as elements of Classical European and Indian musical traditions. His ability to draw inspiration from a variety of musical traditions was also evident on his albums "India," "Ascension," and "A Love Supreme" which was released in 1964 and soon became his most successful recording.

By the late 1960's, Coltrane became a strong supporter of the civil rights movement, he released the song "Alabama," which he wrote in response to the 1963 Birmingham church bombing, which fused his musical, political and cultural consciousness, as he championed racial and social justice.

Anita Baker

Major Awards   **Wins**

Major Awards	Wins
Grammy Awards	8
American Music Awards	4
Soul Train Music Awards	7

Major Hall of Fame Inductions

BET Lifetime Achievement
Hollywood Walk of Fame

Along with her classy, refined brand of romantic Soul music, Singer and Songwriter, Anita Baker (1958 -) was one of the most popular artists in urban contemporary music, a genre that her traditional Soul and R&B singing helped to define in the 1980's and 1990's. Her strong three-octave vocal range, exceptional power in the recording studio and onstage brought her international acclaim. Producing classics hits such as, "Caught up in the Rapture" and "You Bring Me Joy," made her one of the most popular romantic singers of her time. Baker was influenced not only by R&B, but also Jazz, Gospel, and traditional Pop, which gave her music a distinct adult sophistication.

Singer and Songwriter, Anita Baker is regarded as one of the most popular singers of soulful romantic ballads during the height of the Quiet Storm period of contemporary R&B in the 1980's. Growing up in Detroit, Michigan, her talent first became apparent when she began singing in church choir at the age of 12. She was inspired to sing and perform by listening to female Jazz singers like Sarah Vaughan, Nancy Wilson and Ella Fitzgerald. By the age of 16, she was performing with several local bands.

In 1975, Baker joined the group named "Chapter 8," which was one of Detroit's most popular groups during the time. In 1982, Otis Smith, (who was an executive producer who worked with Chapter 8 on a few hit songs) contacted Baker about recording for his new label, "Beverly Glen Records." She flew out to California to record her debut album, "The Songstress" (1983). The album spent more than a year on the charts, while also helping Baker build a strong fan base. In 1985, she then signed with label "Elektra Records," and threw herself wholeheartedly into her next project.

Baker supervised every aspect of the record's production. Filling the role of executive producer herself, a nearly unprecedented move for a rising star at the time (she chose "The Songstress" collaborator Michael Powell as producer). They succeeded brilliantly and released her first major record label debut, "Rapture" (1986). The album was a massive hit, selling 5 million copies worldwide and appealing to both urban and adult contemporary listeners and producing three all-time Quiet Storm classics in "Sweet Love" "Caught Up in the Rapture" and "You Bring Me Joy."

Her equally stylish follow-up album, "Giving You the Best That I Got," was released in 1988, spawning more staples with the title track and "Just Because." The album was an immediate success, topping the Billboard charts and selling more than 8 million copies worldwide. For her next 2 albums, Baker decided to handle a greater share of the songwriting and production process, hence the title "Compositions," which was released in 1990, she also incorporated more Jazz elements than in previous albums.

The album launched the singles "Talk to Me," "Soul Inspiration" and "Fairy Tales," selling over one million copies. Four years later, she returned to the charts with "Rhythm of Love" featuring her signature song "Body and Soul."

Johnny Mathis

Major Awards   **Wins**

R&B Pioneer Award   1
Guinness World Record   1

Major Hall of Fame Inductions

Grammy Hall of Fame
Hit Parade Hall of Fame
Songwriter's Hall of Fame
Hollywood Walk of Fame

Widely known as "The Voice of Romance," Legendary singer, Johnny Mathis (1935 -) is truly one of the music industry's most treasured voices. Along with a massive fan base, Mathis has endured longevity throughout his career scoring a hit record in six consecutive decades. Best known for his supremely popular hit songs such as "Chances Are," "It's Not For Me To Say," and "Misty," Mathis has recorded more than 80 albums, which includes 6 Christmas albums, and has sold more than 350 million records worldwide. As an artist, he ranks No. 6 in the all-time history of Billboard's Pop album charts. He is "Columbia Records" longest running recording artist. In 1958, he became the first artist in history to release a "Greatest Hits" album, this created a new category of music that has become an industry standard since its introduction.

Singer and Songwriter, commonly referred to as "The Voice of Romance," or "The Velvet Voice," Johnny Mathis is recognized as one of the greatest vocalist of the 20th century. As a native of Texas, he was raised in San Francisco, California. His vocal talent was recognized at 8 years old, his father then hired him a vocal coach. While in high school, he also was talented enough at track and field to get an athletic scholarship to San Francisco State University, and later, an invitation to try out for the U.S. team heading to the 1956 Summer Olympics in Melbourne, Australia.

Mathis also often took part in San Francisco's famous "Black Hawk Nightclub" jam sessions, in 1955, the clubs owner, Helen Noga noticed his singing talent at one of these sessions and began scheduling him weekly. During one of his performances, Mathis was offered a recording contract with "Columbia Records." On his father's advice he decided to pursue a musical career rather than compete in the Olympic tryouts that year. In 1956, he recorded his first Jazz album, "Johnny Mathis: a New Sound in Popular Song."

Columbia Records Vice President Mitch Miller then persuaded Mathis to focus on romantic Jazz ballads. In 1956, he recorded his first hit song, "Wonderful! Wonderful!" which sold more than one million records, it was soon followed by the single "It's Not for Me to Say." MGM Studios signed Mathis to sing that song in the 1957 motion picture "Lizzie." Shortly after, 20th Century Fox contracted Mathis to sing in its film "A Certain Smile." Before the year ended Mathis recorded two other hits, "Chances Are" and "The Twelfth of Never," and appeared on The Ed Sullivan Show.

The national exposure between television and films ensured stardom for Mathis who was now being referred to as "The Velvet Voice." In 1958, he achieved another distinction with his album "Johnny's Greatest Hits" which was the first greatest hits album released in the music industry, it also became one of the best-selling albums in Columbia Records history.

Along with a legendary career that has spanned over six decades, Mathis has been honored to make several appearances before various heads of state, including command performances for two U.S. Presidents, the British Royal Family, the President of Liberia and the Prime Minister of Japan.

Billy Eckstine

<u>Major Hall of Fame Inductions</u>

Grammy Lifetime Achievement
Grammy Hall of Fame

Known as "Mr. B." Billy Eckstine (1914 - 1993) was a multi-talented Jazz musician, Pop singer and Bandleader who gained popularity during the early 1940's. His smooth and distinctive vocals broke down barriers early in his career, first as leader of the original "Bop Big Band," then as the first romantic African-American male in popular music. Eckstine was also a huge influence in the cultural development of Soul and R&B. In the mid-1940's, he turned to solo vocal recordings and had a stream of hits including "Blowing the Blues Away," "Everything I Have is Yours," "Blue Moon," "Caravan," and "I Apologize." Considered to be the first Bop Big Band, "The Billy Eckstine Orchestra" released the chart-topping singles "A Cottage for Sale" and "Prisoner of Love" in 1945, each sold one million copies, which was a groundbreaking accomplishment during that era.

Jazz Musician and Pop Singer commonly referred to as "Mr. B." Billy Eckstine was one of the most influential Bandleaders and Pop stars of the 20th century. Growing up in Pittsburgh, Pennsylvania, Eckstine began singing at the age of 7, his family then relocated to Washington D.C. where he later attended Howard University. After only a year of college, he won first place in an amateur music contest at the Howard Theater and decided to pursue a professional singing career.

Eckstine began performing in nightclubs along with dance bands. In 1939, he became the lead singer in "Earl Hines Big Band," they soon began recording classics such as "Jelly, Jelly" and "Skylark," which both became national hit records. Although a proficient trombonist, Eckstine also learned how to play the trumpet. In 1943, he recruited a trio of stellar bandmates such as newcomers, Dizzy Gillespie, Charlie Parker, and Sarah Vaughan.

After forming his own big band the same year, Eckstine hired all three and gradually recruited more legendary figures such as Miles Davis and Dexter Gordon. After breaking through several barriers, (considered as the Jackie Robinson of popular music) Eckstine achieved great personal success while fostering the careers of a number of younger Jazz musicians.

Eckstine's band introduced rhythmic and melodic innovations that transformed the standard Jazz of the 1920's, primarily from steady dance music to Bebop, (A music of offbeat accents and orchestral improvisations). Although other big bands experimented with the new sounds, Eckstine's band was the first group to highlight them, and he was credited with forming the original "Bop Big Band."

In the mid-1940s, Eckstine turned to solo vocal recordings and signed with the newly established "MGM Records." He had an immediate stream of hit singles including "Blowing the Blues Away" "Everything I Have is Yours," "Blue Moon," "Caravan," and "I Apologize," which sold millions of copies. By 1950, he was MGM's top-selling Pop singer and was drawing record-breaking concert crowds at the "Oasis Club" in Los Angeles as well as New York's Paramount Theater and Carnegie Hall. For his trailblazing career as a pioneer and legendary performer, Eckstine's home where he grew up later received a State historical marker in his hometown of Pittsburgh.

Roberta Flack

Major Awards	Wins
Grammy Awards	4
American Music Award	1

Major Hall of Fame Inductions

Grammy Lifetime Achievement
Grammy Hall of Fame
North Carolina Music Hall of Fame

Internationally hailed as one of the greatest vocalists of the 20th century, Roberta Flack (1937 -) remains unparalleled in her ability to tell a story through her music. Her songs bring insight into people through life, culture and politics, while effortlessly crossing over a broad musical landscape from Pop to Soul, and Folk to Jazz. Flack is the only solo artist in history to win a Grammy Award for "Record of the Year" for 2 consecutive years, 1973 and 1974. Recognizing the influence music has on the world, she founded "The Roberta Flack School of Music" at The Hyde Leadership Charter School in the Bronx, New York, which provides an innovative and inspiring music education program to underprivileged students free of charge. Throughout her career, Flack has inspired an entire generation of musical legends with her musical brilliance and honesty.

Singer, Songwriter and Pianist renowned for her smooth, "Velvety" voice, Roberta Flack is considered one of the best all around Jazz, Soul, R&B, and Folk music singers of the 1970's. Growing up in Arlington, Virginia, both her parents played the organ in church. Flack was exposed to Gospel music from an early age, as Gospel legend Mahalia Jackson sang at another church across the street from her house. Musically gifted as a child, Flack began taking piano lessons at 9 years old, at the age of 13 she won second prize in a piano competition for African-American students.

In 1952 at the age of 15 she enrolled at Howard University on a full music scholarship. In doing so, she became the youngest student to enroll in that institution in the 20th century. Within a year, she was conducting her sorority's (Delta Sigma Theta) vocal quartet and accompanying Pop, Jazz and Opera singers while they were touring Washington D.C. Flack began taking voice lessons, concentrating primarily on Opera music.

Flack was discovered while singing at a Washington, D.C. nightclub "Mr. Henry's" by Jazz musician Les McCann, he then offered to arrange a meeting with "Atlantic Records." She performed 42 songs within three hours for producer Joel Dorn, she was immediately signed to a contract in 1968. Her entire first album "First Take" was recorded within an unprecedented 10 hours.

She then began releasing a string of hits including, "The First Time Ever I Saw Your Face," "Where Is the Love," "Killing Me Softly With His Song," and her signature song, "The Closer I Get to You" (A romantic ballad recorded with Soul singer and fellow Howard classmate Donny Hathaway). Her slow sensual versions of songs helped usher in a new style of Soulful Pop music. She became the only solo artist in history to win a Grammy Award for "Record of the Year" for 2 consecutive years, 1973 and 1974.

Flack continued to hit Billboard charts several times over the next few years. In 1983, she partnered with singer Peabo Bryson, (with whom she toured in 1980) to record the hit duet "Tonight, I Celebrate My Love." She spent the remainder of the 1980's touring and performing (often with orchestras) several times with Jazz legend Miles Davis. Over the course of her legendary career that has spanned more than five decades, she has released 19 albums.

Kenneth "BabyFace" Edmonds

Major Awards	Wins
Grammy Awards	11
American Music Awards	3
Soul Train Awards	4
NAACP Image Awards	2
BMI Icon Award	1
Trumpet Award	1

Major Hall of Fame Inductions

Hollywood Walk of Fame
Songwriter's Hall of Fame

Kenneth "Babyface" Edmonds (1959 -) has emerged as one
of the most prolific producers, songwriters, and performers in popular
music. Much of his early success has been achieved in partnership
with record executive, Antonio "L.A." Reid, with whom they founded the
"LaFace Records" label in 1989, the duo was responsible for hundreds
of R&B chart-topping hit records from various artists during the late
20th century. As an architect of the Pop scene for over three decades,
Edmonds has written songs for such Pop luminaries as Michael
Jackson, Whitney Houston, Boyz II Men, Aretha Franklin and Vanessa
Williams. Edmonds, who was given the nickname Babyface by
guitarist Bootsy Collins, has also had a legendary career as a solo
recording artist.

Singer, Songwriter and Producer, Kenneth "Babyface" Edmonds was an inescapable presence in virtually every major facet of Pop music during the 1980's and 1990's. His recordings helped rejuvenate the R&B tradition of the smooth, sensitive and urban contemporary sound. Growing up in Indianapolis, Indiana, he began playing the guitar in a local R&B band at the age of 16. He later played with Funk performer Bootsy Collins, who nicknamed him "Babyface" because of his youthful look. Edmonds then joined the Funk band "Manchild," who signed a record deal in 1977, and released 3 albums.

Manchild then broke up as a group after 2 years, Edmonds and drummer, Antonio "L.A." Reid then formed a Funk group called "The Deele," they scored several hits on the R&B charts in the early 1980's. Edmonds and Reid began producing and writing songs for other artists during the release The Deele's third album in 1988. The duo then co-founded "LaFace Records" in 1989. As the decade progressed, Edmonds and Reid then launched a number of successful new acts, most notably Johnny Gill and TLC.

While writing and producing for other artists as a part of LaFace, Edmonds was also working on his solo career. In 1989, his solo album, "Tender Lover," which featured the hit single "Whip Appeal" sold over 2 million copies. The 1992 movie soundtrack to the Eddie Murphy film "Boomerang" featured a song Edmonds wrote titled "End of the Road," for R&B group, Boyz II Men, the single spent 13 weeks at No. 1 on the Billboard charts and became one of the best-selling singles in history. He also wrote and produced the soundtrack for the 1995 motion picture "Waiting to Exhale," which featured several hit songs, most notably Whitney Houston performing "Shoop Shoop." Beginning in 1996, he was awarded the Grammy Award for "Producer of The Year" for 3 consecutive years.

Edmonds has crafted some of the most consistently appealing music in contemporary Pop and R&B. Respected for his talents in capturing the warmth and vitality of the female voice, he conceived several projects to showcase a range of great R&B women, from legends such as Aretha Franklin, Patti LaBelle, Chaka Kahn and Mary J. Blige. Throughout his legendary career as a songwriter, producer and solo artist, he has sold over 200 million records worldwide.

Sources

African-American Inventions That Changed The World:
Today in African-American History: Michael A. Carson.
Autobiography of African-American music, Samuel Top
Carson, Mary Carson, Lydia Morris, Margaret Hall, Willie Hall,
Guinness World Records, Rock & Roll Hall of Fame, Pulitzer
Prize for Music, Grammy Hall of Fame, Soul Train Hall of
Fame, Songwriter's Hall of Fame, Apollo Theater Hall of
Fame, Georgia Music Hall of Fame, Blues Hall of Fame,
National Women's Hall of Fame, Soul Music Hall of Fame,
Country Music Hall of Fame, Grammy Awards, American
Music Awards, NAACP Image Awards, Academy Awards,
Emmy Awards, Golden Globe Awards, Tony Awards, BET
Awards, R&B Pioneer Awards, UNCF Trumpet Award,
Country Music Awards, Grammy Lifetime Achievement,
Hollywood Walk of Fame, St. Louis Walk of Fame, U.K. Music
Hall of Fame, R&B Hall of Fame, Gospel Music Hall of Fame,
Christian Music Hall of Fame, NAACP Hall of Fame, Vocal
Group Hall of Fame, Big Band Hall of Fame, Jazz Hall of
Fame, Apollo Legends Hall of Fame, Chicago Blues Hall of
Fame, Dance Music Hall of Fame, NAACP Spingarn Medal,
National Medal of Arts, Billboard Music Awards, MTV Video
Music Awards, World Music Awards, Presidential Medal of
Freedom, U.S Postal Service, BET Lifetime Achievement,
Museum of African Diaspora, San Francisco, CA. African-
American Museum of History and Culture, Washington, D.C.

ACKNOWLEDGEMENTS

As always, I have to begin by giving thanks to God, for guiding my life and giving my family and I his infinite blessings.

To my lovely wife Shenika and our son Matthew.

To my parents, Mary and Sam, who gave me life and taught me how to love God and Family.

To my sister and brother-in-law, Sandra and Arthur.
To my brother and sister-in-law, Sanford and Brigette.
Thank you for your love and support.

To my nieces and nephews, Serena, Stephanie, Shayla, Jayda, Keiana, Darin, Darius and Austin.

To the entire Carson, Street, Hall and Bolden families.
Much love to all of you.

About The Authors

Michael and Matthew Carson are a Best-Selling, Award-Winning Father and Son writing team. They are most well known for their publications: "African-American Inventions That Changed The World" and "Today In African-American History."

Growing up in Queens, New York, Michael has a Bachelors Degree in Psychology from Virginia State University and works as a Government Analyst. Matthew is an elementary school student who enjoys researching and writing about history. Their family currently resides in Atlanta, Georgia.

What began a conversation with Michael teaching his son Matthew about African-American history, continued into a three book non-fiction series. Together their passion for learning about historical figures grew into a collaboration, and they wanted to educate future generations about the many significant contributions African-Americans have made in our society and the world.

Michael and his wife Shenika co-founded Double Infinity Publishing. Their goal is to publish high quality literature that represents historical facts as well as provide a voice and platform for educating readers.

Made in the USA
Columbia, SC
31 March 2021